"This book gets to the heart of how to best support teachers in helping even their most challenging students. Combining their knowledge and experience as an ADHD expert and a special education teacher, Cindy Goldrich and Carly Wolf provide real, practical, and powerful insights and tools. This book is invaluable for all classroom teachers."

— **Edward Hallowell, MD**,
author of *Driven to Distraction*

"Starting from a strengths-based approach, this book has easy to understand explanations of issues that may arise when working with students who have ADHD and EF challenges. It's full of fantastic activities & worksheets that focus on honing essential skills like time management, taking someone else's perspective, flexible thinking, and developing grit, and is perfect for the classroom teacher short on time who needs ready to go resources."

— **Janine Halloran, LMHC**,
author of *Coping Skills for Kids Workbook*

"Both personally, as a parent, and professionally, as head of our school district's foundation, I have seen how transformative Cindy's work can be! Her tips, tools and strategies for parents and educators consistently prove to help adults understand and support kids with ADHD and related challenges. The outcomes speak for themselves."

— **Allison Billings**,
Executive Director, Impact on Education

"Stress and anxiety have reached a crisis point in our school and home environments. Tools are no longer optional, they are now a requirement for every teacher. This exceptional team of experts have put these skills into practice both in the classroom and in the field. Join this mother-daughter team in implementing these excellent hands-on tools and techniques that support students in finding the peace in their challenges and empowering them to thrive in all areas of life."

— **Elenn Steinberg**,
Founder and Executive Director, Every Child Reading

"This book is an invaluable guide for educators as well as an essential resource for parents. For many years, I have seen Cindy work with teachers of students with ADHD from Kindergarten through 12th grade, as well as with our Child Study Team members and parents. Today, parents and teachers alike are often overwhelmed. I have witnessed first-hand the appreciation any adult who cares about any child has for her expertise and guidance. Her work is a breath of fresh air for any adult who cares for any child."

— **Richard Cohen**,
Assistant Superintendent of Metuchen School
District and Principal of Moss School

"Wow! I wish I could put this book in the hands of every teacher. Not only does it make the academic topic of executive function accessible, it translates the best research-backed methods for developing these critical skills into clear, actionable strategies for the classroom. This book is a gift to all educators - and the children they support."

— **Krista Marks**,
CEO of Woot Tutor and former Vice President of Disney Online

"*ADHD, Executive Function and Behavioral Challenge in the Classroom* is a much-needed resource. It provides children with the tools needed to help transform common challenges related to ADHD, and is a resource to educators who struggle with how to breakthrough with their students in the classroom. Cindy Goldrich and Carly Wolf provide a clear explanation along with useful and straight forward exercises to help set up the child for success."

— **Melissa Springstead Cahill, PsyD, MFT**,
author of *ADHD in Teens & Young Adults*

"This book is a powerhouse of in-depth and practical information on helping students with executive functioning deficits in the classroom. Its exploration of how to handle each aspect of executive functioning is outstanding. I wish our program had had this resource for our long-term school training programs."

— **Maureen A. Gill, LCSW, ACC**

"This well-written and insightful book helps educators and others by providing new strategies and tools to better understand and reach and teach students with neurobehavioral challenges. It empowers and connects teachers with fresh perspectives to better understand and engage students to promote academic successes. The many user-friendly worksheets are practical and fun, and will help students better know and challenge themselves to stretch and master the skills they need. This book will energize and inspire students and teachers. Highly recommended."

— **Gene Carroccia, PsyD, Clinical Psychologist**,
author of *Treating ADHD/ADD in Children and Adolescents*

"We have the technology, and we know icebergs are much bigger than they appear on the surface. Cindy Goldrich is an ADHD thought leader because she understands there is more to ADHD and executive functioning challenges than how they appear! She also understands the importance and power of connection and collaboration. Her book and training programs emphasize the importance of connection and collaboration to help teachers and professionals understand the invisible drivers that lead to success in helping those impacted by ADHD!"

— **Jeff Copper, PCC**,
ADHD coach, host of Attention Talk Radio

ADHD,
Executive Function & Behavioral Challenges
in the
Classroom

Managing the Impact on
Learning, Motivation, and Stress

Cindy Goldrich, EdM, ADHD-CCSP & Carly Wolf, BS, Ed

Published by
PESI Publishing
PESI, Inc
3839 White Ave
Eau Claire, WI 54703

Cover: Amy Rubenzer
Editing: Jenessa Jackson, PhD
Layout: Amy Rubenzer & Bookmasters

ISBN: 9781683732297

Printed in the United States of America.

PESI Publishing
pesipublishing.com

About the Author

Cindy Goldrich, EdM, ADHD-CCSP, is a mental health counselor, parent coach, and teacher trainer. She is a nationally recognized expert for parents and professionals who deal with the complex challenges created by ADHD, executive function challenges, anxiety, and learning disabilities. Cindy is the author of *8 Keys for Parenting Children with ADHD* and the creator of the Calm and Connected: Parent the Child You Have© workshop series offered on-demand and via live workshops offered nationwide. She is the founder of PTScoaching.com that offers coaching and training for parents and professionals worldwide.

Carly Wolf, BS, Ed, is a special education teacher. She received her master's in special education as an intervention specialist with a focus in academic coaching and leadership from the University of Northern Colorado. She received her bachelor degree in elementary and special education from the University of Delaware. Just after graduating from University of Delaware, Carly moved to Boulder, Colorado, where she is currently a Special Education teacher.

Dedication

As we learn more about the impacts of social-emotional learning on educational adeptness, the pressures on teachers to be much more than educators has become overwhelming. We want to acknowledge and support the incredible teachers who work tirelessly to educate our next generation. Most teachers go into this profession with the pure and honorable intention of helping children learn and grow. Today's teachers are now also charged with dealing with expectations and stressors from all around them (parents, administrators, and society) at a greater rate than ever before. We dedicate this book to them – for their love, care, efforts, and commitment to make a difference for every student.

I am proud and honored to have had the opportunity to collaborate on this book with my daughter, Carly. She chose early in life to pursue a career as a special education teacher. I have seen her grow and develop into a mature and compassionate person and professional, full of insight and wisdom beyond her years. They say from your children you will be taught, and on a daily basis, this has been true for me. Beyond our mother and daughter bond, ours is a true professional partnership of learning, sharing, and growing as we work to help children, parents, and professionals understand one another and thrive together.

Cindy Goldrich

The process of writing this book has been a beautiful and collaborative effort between mother and daughter. Our process has been the work of melding our experience and expertise together. I have treasured the growing professional bond we have developed leading up to and through this process.

I also want to dedicate this book to my husband-to-be, Daniel. Thank you for teaching me and inspiring me every day with the incredible work you do with your own students. I cherish our shared conversations around our daily challenges in the classroom and the ways that we help each other grow. You are a gift to every single one of your students. Thank you for supporting me through this process and allowing me to make it all happen. I am so lucky to have you in my life.

Carly Wolf

Table of Contents

6.

Helping Students Develop Grit

7.

The Power of Student Goal Setting

Introduction

This book is a collaborative effort between Cindy—an ADHD clinician specializing in parent coaching and teacher training—and Carly—a special education teacher. We work hands-on with students, classroom teachers, related service providers, and parents to help each party understand the struggles faced by students with attention-deficit/hyperactivity disorder (ADHD) and executive function challenges, as well as to help each group understand the other's experiences. An essential trust must be built for students, teachers, and parents to be able to work well together, and our success has been based on helping each group deeply appreciate one another's struggles.

We have written this book with teachers in mind, though the information we share will provide practical supports to anyone working with a child who is struggling in the classroom. **In this book, we share the insights, tools, and activities that we have found to make a profound impact on the education of children who learn differently.** In writing this book together, we share a unique bond not only as mother and daughter but also as professional colleagues, sounding boards, and mutual mentors.

WHO ARE WE?

Cindy

My work as both a parent coach and a teacher trainer has given me a unique viewpoint regarding how each group's needs and perspectives impact the others. I have provided professional development and parent coaching to thousands of people across the country. I have worked with teachers, guidance counselors, occupational therapists, speech/language pathologists, social workers, school psychologists, paraprofessionals, and principals— educating them about the impact ADHD and executive function challenges have on students' ability to access and utilize knowledge. As a parent coach, I've benefited from a behind-the-scenes view of the struggles parents and students often face as they work to manage school expectations. Incorporating the teachers' perspective and constraints has allowed me to guide parents by providing realistic, useful feedback—as well as consulting—to effectively integrate teachers' concerns and agendas. Working with both professionals and parents has allowed me to create a circle of support for all involved.

Carly

As a resource room teacher, I have worked collaboratively with students, general education teachers, and parents to help students be successful in all school settings. I have developed strategies with my students to help them generalize the skills they have learned with me regarding stress management and executive functioning. I have provided support for teachers to help them manage accommodations and modifications identified in Individualized Educational Plans (IEPs) and 504 plans, as well as to manage the behavioral challenges their students face. As a teacher, I value the insights that I've gained regarding the many challenges that parents face at home with their children. We are all here with the same goal: to help our students be successful. By gaining an understanding of how some of the challenges we see at school manifest at home, I have been able to better help both teachers and parents in supporting each other to best meet the needs of our students.

HOW DO WE BEST SUPPORT OUR STUDENTS?

Together, our experiences have convinced us wholeheartedly that the opportunity to make a positive change in our schools and for our kids is ripe, and that educators and related professionals are hungry—in fact, desperate— for these changes to happen now. In addition to teaching math, science, social studies, and language arts, more and more general education teachers are being asked to be behaviorists and interventionists—a job they were not necessarily trained to do. By incorporating social and emotional learning into the classroom in subtle and consistent ways, we are finding that students are developing a greater awareness of and ability to manage their self-regulation skills, which reduces the overall level of stress in the classroom.

In the introduction to her first book, *8 Keys to Parenting Children with ADHD*, Cindy suggests that parents should learn to "parent the child you have." In other words, they should develop realistic expectations about how to best parent the child they were blessed with—not the child they *thought* they would have, not the child they *wished* they had, and not the one they would have if their mother-in-law got her way. For children who exhibit complex and challenging behaviors, parenting with traditional love, logic and intuition is not enough to help these children thrive. Parents need education about the impact of their child's unique challenges and a parenting strategy that is tailored to the unique needs of their individual child. Well, the same can be said for those of us who work with these kids in the classroom setting: We need a deep understanding of these students so that we may *teach and guide* them, and we need to use specific tools and strategies that are tailored to *each student*.

However, how can we address the unique needs of these students while still keeping the needs of the classroom as a whole in mind? Indeed, having students who learn and perform differently than the majority of students in the classroom *does* create an added burden for already over-taxed teachers. Statistically, the majority of students with ADHD are educated in the mainstream classroom and do not have additional paraprofessionals to help them. This puts the burden on the classroom teacher to put forth additional time and resources to meet the needs of a variety of students. It often means that teachers need greater prep time and that they must modify classroom lessons and activities. **That is where we hope this workbook can help: Our goal is to minimize the time that teachers need to spend with any one individual student so that they can maximize their effectiveness with all of their students.**

HOW TO MAKE THE BEST USE OF THIS BOOK

Have you ever tried to help a friend learn a new skill or assemble a newly purchased item, and he or she just wants to dive in without reading the instructions? (We know, some of you *are* that friend!) Sometimes, pushing forward without instructions can go smoothly, but other times it becomes a frustrating, ineffective experience because that person doesn't really *understand* the nuances that are at the heart of the matter.

Having conducted full-day trainings for professionals for many years now, the most common feedback Cindy has received is not about the tools that she provides (although those have been greatly appreciated and utilized); rather, it is about the new perspective and insight that professionals have gained regarding the **real** impact of ADHD and executive dysfunction on children's learning, motivation, and behavior. By going beyond issues that are the usual focal point (e.g., "How do I get him to focus, listen, be organized, and do his work?"), we have been able to give teachers, mental health professionals, and related service providers a roadmap for understanding how these kids tick. Professionals have then been able to modify any existing tools that they have and "dance in the moment," which effectively creates a new way to reach that child where they need it most.

In writing this workbook, we have selected our favorite and most user-friendly charts, worksheets, activities, and tools for you to use for yourself, your students, and their parents. The book is divided into the following broad areas:

- Building students' executive function skills
- Enhancing communication and collaboration skills
- Reducing stress in the classroom
- Helping students develop grit and perseverance
- Supporting parents in being effective supports for their children

While we know it is tempting to jump right to the "practical" information, we strongly recommend that you read through the first two chapters: ADHD: Beyond the Basics and What Are Executive Functions. Think of these chapters as your "instructions" for knowing how to build a stronger, more resilient student. The remaining chapters are your tools and materials. Although there is a logical sequence to the way we ordered the remaining chapters, it is not as essential for you to read these sequentially if there is a particular area of support you need.

Within each chapter, we provide the rationale for using a particular tool or activity along with the relevant list, chart, or directions. If, at any time, you find that a particular tool or strategy is not working as you had anticipated or hoped, then you may find it helpful to go back to the first two chapters and ask yourself, "I wonder why?" as you rediscover the uniqueness that each child presents. Even better, wonder out loud with the student you are looking to support. Sometimes his or her own insights are the most valuable of all.

BEFORE WE GET STARTED

Before we talk about how ADHD and executive function challenges impact learning, motivation, and behavior, we want you to think for a moment about how you may have referred to "those kids" when you were growing up, who (in retrospect) may have had ADHD. Not the formal descriptions that were used to describe these kids; rather, the labels that they were often given by peers and others. Words we hear when we ask this question often include "hyper," "troublemaker," "lazy," "space cadet," "class clown," "unmotivated," "difficult," and "crazy"—to name a few. Sadly, some of these descriptions are still used today on the playground and in social gatherings.

Although some people still refer to this condition as ADD, that terminology is no longer accurate. Indeed, according to the official diagnostic criteria in the *Diagnostic and Statistical Manual of Mental Disorders* (DSM), it has been called ADHD since 1987. And do you know what it was called before it was even officially labeled as ADD? Until 1968, it was known as "Minimal brain dysfunction." We know—ugh!

We have come a long way, but we still have a long way to go. In fact, we don't like to think of ADHD as a "disorder" anymore. Our brains are *all* different, with unique strengths, weaknesses, and nuances. The cut-off for many diagnoses is, while based on well-thought-out research and criteria, still somewhat arbitrary. Labels such as ADHD, are helpful and necessary in that they give us a common language to describe a set of symptoms and also help us determine eligibility for certain services. However, our goal is to find ways to discuss and illustrate how certain traits can create specific challenges, as well as opportunities. We choose to use a strength-based approach in looking at what is serving a student well and where we need to provide support.

1. ADHD: Beyond the Basics

ADHD IS REAL!

Across the literature, a variety of imaging studies have demonstrated differences in the structure and activity between brains of people with and without ADHD. People with ADHD, have a consistent pattern of below-normal activity in the neurotransmission of dopamine and norepinephrine in the brain's prefrontal cortex, which is the part of the brain that controls our ability to maintain alertness, focus attention, and sustain thought, effort, and motivation. Importantly, dopamine plays a large role in the brain's reward and pleasure system. Therefore, individuals with ADHD—who have lower levels of dopamine overall—experience under-stimulation in the reward and motivation centers of their brain. So, if you have ever wondered why behavior modification programs involving sticker charts don't seem to work for some kids, this might be part of the reason. Unless these children are intrinsically motivated, the external reward provided by the sticker may not work once the novelty wears off.

Here are a few more general things to know about ADHD that will help how you view your students. While there are still significantly more boys diagnosed with ADHD each year than girls, it appears that this gender gap is not as significant as it once was believed to be. When it comes to ADHD, girls tend to display more symptoms of inattentiveness rather than hyperactivity and impulsivity. Therefore, their symptoms are less likely to be observed by teachers because inattentiveness is less disruptive in the classroom setting. In addition, women are more likely to cope with their ADHD symptoms by masking or internalizing them. In turn, they can become anxious and depressed, leading to a missed diagnosis or a misdiagnosis. The ADHD is not identified. So, keep an eye on those quiet girls. They may seem like they are doing fine, but they may be experiencing some of the same challenges as boys with more overt symptoms.

Another common misconception is that ADHD is merely a childhood disorder that individuals will "grow out of." However, there is evidence that many individuals with ADHD will carry these symptoms into adulthood. The disorder persists into adulthood in approximately 40% to 65% of cases diagnosed in childhood. So, a "wait and see" approach is not always in the child's best interest. At the November 2018 International Conference on ADHD, Russell Barkley, a leading authority in the field, gave a powerful keynote presentation titled *Advances in Understanding the Symptoms of ADHD*. He outlined the numerous and potentially serious impairments that ADHD can have on major life activities. He showed that, when ADHD is not properly treated and managed, people do not learn to regulate their moods, impulses, and actions. This makes them more susceptible to health issues (not properly managing weight, exercise, alcohol, drugs), anxiety, depression, risky behaviors, lower academic achievement, and occupational and financial difficulties. Delaying a diagnosis of ADHD may result in a loss of valuable time in teaching skills, and it can also lead the child to develop a negative self-image.

Is It Attention Deficit?

One of the greatest misconceptions about ADHD is that it renders a person unable to pay attention. In fact, many times we look at a student and say, "He can't have ADHD! He can spend hours… [building, reading, drawing, playing video games, etc.]." However, what science has taught us is that because of the below-normal activity in the neurotransmission of dopamine and norepinephrine, some people with ADHD struggle to regulate their attention. People with ADHD can pay attention, but not always when they need to, for as long as they need to, or on what they need to—especially when they are not interested or internally motivated. This has even led some professionals to suggest that ADHD should be relabeled as "Deficits in Attention Regulation Disorder."

When people with ADHD are bored or uninterested, they struggle to stay tuned in to the current topic and have difficulty resisting more stimulating thoughts. For example, you may see a child looking out the window at the person mowing the lawn, or playing with the loose seam on the textbook even though they know the expectation is to be listening to the teacher. In addition, many people with ADHD are often multi-focused, paying attention to many things at the same time at the expense of directed attention to one thought. They may even feel that they have a bombardment of thoughts, making it difficult to focus on any one task.

On the flip side, when a student with ADHD is very interested in what they're doing (such as playing a video game or building with blocks), that student may actually be hyper-focused. The experience of hyper-focus refers to being so deeply and intensely focused to the point that a person shuts out other thoughts or stimuli. The focus is so intense that the person can become lost in that activity for hours (or days) on end. When students with ADHD experience hyper-focus, it may seem as if they are listening to you, but their attention is miles away.

Therefore, ADHD is, in fact, not a condition that involves deficits in attention; rather, it is one that involves challenges in the regulation of attention. This difficulty in regulating attention is one reason why students with ADHD often have a hard time transitioning from one task to another. We will address some specific strategies for transitioning between strategies in Chapter 2 when we discuss the executive functions.

What Is ADHD?

ADHD is considered a neurodevelopmental disorder of the brain's self-management system. According to the *DSM-5*, it involves a persistent pattern of inattention and/or hyperactivity-impulsivity that interferes with functioning or development (p. 59). The diagnostic criteria indicate that a child needs to exhibit several noticeable inattentive or hyperactive-impulsive symptoms in two or more settings by age 12 (and as early as age 4), and these symptoms must be present for at least six months.

These diagnostic requirements raise some important considerations. First, have you ever had a parent approach you and say, "I'm having such a hard time with Jonny at home. I can't seem to get him to do any of his work"? However, in your mind, Jonny has been doing just fine. Or, perhaps you call a meeting with Sara's parents to discuss some of your concerns with her in the classroom, and her parents indicate that Sara does just fine at home and suggest that maybe her issues lie with the school. As you will see, there are many reasons why ADHD shows up differently in different settings, so it's important not to make judgments or assumptions but rather to understand where shifts and changes need to be made in each setting.

Second, the fact that teachers and parents may have different responses about a child's performance also raises another critical issue regarding perspective. ADHD is highly hereditable. According to a study done on twins, the estimated rate of heritability of ADHD is 0.76 on a scale where 0 means genes have no apparent influence, and scores closer to 1 suggest that genes play a major role in a person's vulnerability to the disorder. The implication is that a significant percentage of children diagnosed with ADHD have at least one parent with ADHD as well. Therefore, when you say to Mr. or Mrs. Smith, "Sara is having a hard time being organized. Can you please help her at home?", there is a good chance that one of Sara's parents is thinking, "And who is going to organize me?" Given this, it is essential to consider how you include parents in supporting your students.

IS ADHD ON THE RISE?

In the 2016 Centers for Disease Control and Prevention study, National Center on Birth Defects and Developmental Disabilities (NCBDDD) scientists indicated that 9.4% of children between 4 and 17 years old living in the U.S. have been diagnosed with ADHD. Since most children with ADHD are educated in the mainstream classroom, this means that there is at least one child with ADHD in most classrooms, regardless of whether that child has an IEP or 504 plan in place. This fact is why we passionately believe that every general education teacher should be adequately trained to understand ADHD. (So, we are grateful that you are reading this book!)

If you have been wondering whether ADHD is on the rise, this statistic is one that we believe is difficult to truly measure. Because there is no agreed upon way to uniformly diagnose ADHD—and because there are no regulations regarding who is qualified to assess the condition (beyond having a medical or mental health license)—there is still some degree of subjectivity involved in terms of who meets the criteria for a diagnosis. However, no doubt teachers are experiencing more challenges in the classroom that look like ADHD, which makes it seem as if the condition is indeed on the rise. We have an alternate explanation:

When you think about kindergarten classes from years ago, they mostly looked like a collection of play centers: a kitchen prep station, dress up area, building station, sand table, etc. Most didn't have chairs, and the crayons were all thick. Most kindergarten classrooms today look rather different. In many schools, there has been a pushdown of curriculum expectations that, in large part, have pushed younger children beyond their developmental ability. The manner in which classrooms are currently structured is in contrast to the past, when there was a greater emphasis on play, with lessons woven in. Why is this so important when it comes to ADHD? Well, it turns out that play serves a vital role in the development of self-regulation skills. Play helps children learn to inhibit their impulsive behavior and follow the rules. It also helps children develop internal dialogue and verbal self-regulation as they have ongoing conversations with others to resolve differences in perspectives, reach agreements about roles, and to invent rules to play by. So perhaps what we are seeing in the classroom is not a rise in ADHD, but rather the reaction of some students who are pushed beyond their developmental abilities. They are being judged as small adults rather than young children.

DON'T STOP THE FIDGETING, TEACH THE TOOL

When children with ADHD have trouble paying attention to the task at hand, sitting still may actually increase the difficulty that they are experiencing. In contrast, engaging in movement can help stimulate the brain regions that control attention by increasing levels of dopamine and norepinephrine in the same way that ADHD medications do. However, when you have a student who is in constant motion, this can create a distraction for you and his or her classmates. One way to help students get the movement they desire while also balancing the need to reduce distractions to other students in the classroom is to use fidgets. Fidgets are a great way to give students who need to keep moving an appropriate tool by which to do this.

Carly likes to keep a bin of different types of fidgets in her classroom for students to use as they wish. We suggest that all classrooms (regardless of grade level) and therapeutic rooms in schools have fidgets available for any student to use. A trip to a novelty or party store can provide some great, inexpensive options for fidgets, such as squeeze balls, pencil toppers, felt, and putty. Some students may also prefer a wearable fidget, like a spinner ring or a bracelet with large movable beads, or even a small piece of cloth that can be held and placed in a pants pocket. Encourage students to experiment to find their own favorite fidget.

It's a good idea to stock up on several different choices since these tools may need to be switched up from time to time to meet the need for novelty that is often a component of ADHD. Indeed, you may have previously tried allowing students to fidget with an object—perhaps a stress ball or some other item—only to find that rather than help them pay attention, it created an additional distraction. That is why it's important to have a variety of options!

When you first introduce fidgets into the classroom, you may find that *all* students will initially start out using the fidgets. However, if taught correctly, only the students who really need them will continue to use the fidgets after a short amount of time. The following series of steps will help you to introduce fidgets to your students and provide them with a set of principles behind the art of fidgeting.

1. **Discuss individual differences in attention.**

   Begin with a full-class discussion about the differences that everyone has regarding the ways they are able to pay attention. What makes it easier for some students to pay attention? Harder? Teach students that science has shown that some people can pay attention more easily when they move around, whereas some find it easier to sit relatively still. There are two essential goals of this conversation. First, we want to help students be more accepting of themselves and others for their differences in terms of how they best focus and learn. There is enough spotlight on "those kids" already. Therefore, rather than only allowing students with IEPs or 504 plans to have fidgets, allow anyone who can use the fidget properly to benefit from having one. Second, we want to raise students' awareness of their *own* best way of being.

2. **Demonstrate the difference between "fidgeting" and "playing."**

   To demonstrating what fidgeting involves, hold an object in your hand (we like to use long rubber sticks called Bendeez for this demonstration), and show students how you can move it quietly in your hands while talking and listening. The object is your secondary focus; it is in the background of your mind. It does not require your attention. You may discretely hold it in your lap under your desk. Next, contrast this with playing with the object. For example, show how you can make it become a pretzel. This action requires your attention, your focus, and your concentration. You are no longer fidgeting. The object is now your primary focus.

3. **Demonstrate respect for others.**

   Show the students what happens when you bang the object on the table or swing it around a bit. Even if you are not bothered by your fidgeting, it can become an annoyance to others. Reinforce the notion that fidgeting involves being respectful and not distracting others in the classroom.

4. **Discuss the rules for fidgeting.**

   These are best generated organically from the class discussion. For example:
   - You may use any safe, small object as a fidget.
   - You need to be quiet when using the fidget.
   - You may not distract others.
   - You may not be destructive when using the fidget.

The chart on the following page can be used to guide discussion around using fidgets appropriately and can be posted in the classroom as a reminder to students.

Is It a Fidget or a Toy?

. . .

Fidget	Toy
Secondary Focus: When a fidget is being used appropriately, it should remain a secondary focus. This means that it should stay in the background of your attention.	**Primary Focus:** A fidget becomes a toy when it is the primary focus of attention rather than what is being taught.
Eyes on Learning: Eyes should remain on the source of learning when fidgets are used correctly. Whether you are completing an independent task or paying attention to the teacher, your focus needs to be on learning.	**Eyes on Fidget:** When eyes are on the fidget instead of the source of learning, it is no longer being used as a fidget. The fidget has now become the primary focus, and attention to the task is lost.
Mindlessly Used: When used properly, a fidget is used mindlessly to the point where it becomes part of a system.	**Actively Used:** When the fidget is actively used, you are investigating how it works, trying to build with it, or trying to create something with it. If a fidget it being actively used, it has now become a toy.

Don't Let Your Fidget Become a Toy!
Be Aware Not to Distract Others!

LET THEM MOVE

As we learn more and more about the benefits of exercise and movement in learning, we are starting to understand the importance of getting our students moving more often during their education. Although some kids are content with fine motor fidgets that they can hold in their hands, other kids have more internal energy that they *need* to use. For them, sitting in a traditional seat for an extended time might be too challenging and restricting. Some kids need to rock, wobble, lean, or even stand to pay attention.

In the younger grades, you may find that many IEPs or 504 plans specify that a student is allowed to sit in a seat that allows for movement. Examples of these types of seats include exercise ball chairs, wobble seats, or seats that have bands around the base of the legs. However, when we speak to parents and teachers of older students, we find that many students are either no longer given the accommodation of flexible seating, or they choose not to take advantage of the opportunity. Why? STIGMA. Students don't want to appear different from their peers. It is not that their need for movement has gone away; it's that they have gained a level of awareness that tells them that their need to move is somehow "abnormal" relative to the rest of their classmates.

Increasingly, we find that businesses have adapted seating options that include swivel chairs, couches, standing desks, and even desks with foot pedals for stationary cycling. Many businesses have open areas for people to gather around small tables, sit on couches, and stand at stools around high tables. Science and experience have clearly shown that sitting all day is generally a bad idea, and having the flexibility to stand and move around makes for a productive work environment.

Aside from creating movement opportunities, allowing students to have flexible seating options enables them to take ownership of their learning and attention in the classroom. It also gives educators an opportunity reduce the potential stigma attached to these different options by teaching and demonstrating that people often require different conditions to be successful. Some students will prefer the traditional desk or table and chair. Other students might appreciate finally having the opportunity to move around as they learn—without standing out. We all need different things to be successful. The traditional desk and chair model is not necessarily ideal for all students.

Most teachers who have flexible seating in their rooms report that they are very pleased with the results. They find that students are more engaged, less resistant, more productive, and more relaxed. The students also take their seating options seriously. In addition, many teachers experience a decrease in discipline problems and an improvement in grades when there is a more comfortable, relaxed environment.

On the following pages, we provide some guidelines and suggestions to help you incorporate flexible seating into your classroom. The objective here is to follow the same principles that were laid out regarding teaching the art of fidgeting. We want to help students learn about themselves, their needs, and their best way of being productive as they learn and work.

Incorporating Flexible Seating into the Classroom

• • •

1. Look at your classroom from a new perspective. Consider the ideal setting and then work from there. Dream big, think broadly, and have fun. You may want to look at photos on the internet for inspiration. Depending on the physical size of your classroom and the number of students in your class, you may need to adjust the options you offer. At this stage, don't worry about cost or availability; we will tackle that soon.

2. Options for seating and working are endless. Consider having places for those who prefer to be more stationary versus those who need to move around more. You can also think about different seating areas for various learning purposes (group activities, quiet work, testing, work with materials, etc.). Regardless of the types of seats you have, it might be enjoyable to have a rug or two, some meditation pillows, a low table, some clipboards, and some lap desks. Below are some ideas on how to transform your classroom into a flexible seating classroom.

   • **Floor Cushions:** Simple floor cushions can be a great way to allow students to sit on the floor. Some students simply learn better if they can sit on the floor or a soft surface.

   • **Wobble Seats:** Wobble seats allow students to improve their posture and build a strong core, which leads to greater motor control. They provide great sensory output as students burn energy in an appropriate and productive manner. Wobble seats also increase blood flow as students wiggle and wobble back and forth. Increased blood flow means that more oxygen gets to the brain, which allows brain function to increase, leading to improved focus and greater retention of knowledge.

   • **Exercise Balls:** Exercise balls hold a lot of the same benefits that wobble seats do, while being more cost-effective overall. To allow for more sturdiness, try placing the exercise ball in crates to help keep them where they are.

   • **Lowered/Raised Tables:** Try seeing if the tables you have in the classroom can be lowered closer to the ground for students who may prefer sitting on the floor. Similarly, raised tables can also be a great option to give students a choice to stand in your classroom.

3. Here are some questions you may want to ask yourself when thinking about how you want your class to look:

   • What type of work do you generally ask of your students?

   • If you require group work, is there usually a need for a large work surface?

   • How many people are typically in a group?

4. While you will need to have students modulate their voices and noise level during group work (as always), think about how closely you can have different work areas placed to one another.

5. Consider the focal point of the room for times when you are conducting full-class discussions and where the smart board or other technology will be set up.

6. Cost, of course, is often one of the biggest concerns. Many teachers have found tremendous success in creating the classrooms of their desire using a combination of the following resources:

   - PTA/PTO

   - Donations of materials from parents, friends, and local businesses

   - Grants

   - Student projects from industrial arts class (commonly referred to as "shop class")

   - Garage sales

   - Online swapping/resale groups

   - DonorChoice.org and other crowdsource funding options

7. Now that you have this beautiful new room with lots of seating options, it will be necessary to help your students adjust to all their choices.

   - Begin by demonstrating all of the seating options and areas. Be sure to set the expectations upfront regarding how seats are to be used, and whether they are allowed to be moved (and if they need to be returned to their original placement).

   - The first week or two, you may want students to rotate through the options, trying each one. They may have certain assumptions, and allowing them to experiment with different options will help them learn which types of seats work best for different situations.

   - Inevitably, some seats or areas may be more popular than others. Develop a system for how the students will have access to the seats. You might consider a rotating schedule or a lottery.

   - Just as with the rules for fidgeting, if students do not initially use the seats correctly, help them understand *why* this is the case (e.g., it is destructive, noisy, distracting), and give them an opportunity to adjust or choose a different option. The goal is always to help them make good choices and be intentional in their decisions.

TIME—IT'S NOW, OR IT'S NOT NOW

Imagine that Jonny's parents call up to him and say, "Hey Jonny, will you please come down for dinner in five minutes?" Five minutes pass by, and Jonny still doesn't come down. What are the assumptions that many parents (and others) make about Jonny? They might say that he's lazy, he doesn't care, he's so involved in what he is doing that he lost track of time, he's defiant, or he's disrespectful. We've heard it all.

Do you know anyone (perhaps a friend, a spouse, a family member, or—dare we say—even yourself) who is chronically late, and who is always surprised at this tardiness? Or maybe you know someone who is always rushing you. Someone who is constantly saying, "Come on, we are going to be late!", while you're thinking, "We have 10 more minutes. What is the rush?" What assumptions do you make in these situations?

While it's natural and typical to make assumptions about people's behavior, when it comes to individuals with ADHD, there is often something else going on as well. This is not to say that some of these assumptions are not true at one time or another.

Research has shown that the ability to estimate the passage of time is weaker for people with ADHD and does not improve when they are on stimulant medication (Barkley, Koplowitz, Anderson, & McMurray, 1997). It turns out that some people's internal clock is not as accurate as other people's. They don't *feel* the passage of time in the same way. Therefore, their whole sense of time is skewed. Importantly, this difficulty in estimating time doesn't just result from their inattention to the present moment; it also results from their inattention to the *future*. As Dr. Edward Hallowell put it, "In the world of ADD, there are only two times: *now* and *not now*" (2011, p. 92).

Consider how this "now" or "not now" mentality can impact students in your classroom. Imagine that you tell the class on Monday, "Okay everyone, there will be a math test on Friday." In turn, Jonny thinks, "Why are we talking about that now? The fire's not at the door yet." After all, "If tomorrow is not the DUE date, then today is not the DO date."

This brings us to a vital message: Whenever you are giving students a task that must be completed within a certain timeframe, you must provide them with *something* to measure time with. Often, teachers assume that having a clock present in the classroom is sufficient. However, this is not the case! If you tell your students, "Okay, you have 10 minutes to complete this assignment," don't assume that they are looking at the clock and saying to themselves, "Hmm, it's 10:05, so I have to be done by 10:15." On the contrary, many students need more direct support to measure the passage of time.

One way to more concretely help support students estimate the passage of time is through the use of visual timers. We have had tremendous success using these devices. Visual timers do not necessarily focus on the overall or absolute time but, instead, help visually display the amount of time remaining for a given task. When you tell your students that they have 10 minutes for a given assignment, you can set the timer for 10 minutes, and they will see time disappearing. **The following page provides some suggestions for making the best use of visual timers.**

Visual Timers

· · ·

1. Regardless of grade level, we suggest that each classroom and therapeutic setting has several visual timers available so that students can have them near their work area. That way it is not just a device for "those" kids with special needs; rather, it is a tool that anyone can benefit from. In fact, students whom you least suspect might be the ones who utilize this tool most often.

2. Discuss with the class that not everyone has the same awareness of the passage of time. We are each responsible for knowing how much time we have to complete tasks, arrive somewhere, or stop an activity in order to go on to another activity. You may want to tie in a discussion about transitioning between activities, as discussed in Chapter 2.

3. Each time you assign a task that has a time limit, make sure that you either set one timer that the whole class can see, or strategically place a few around the room to ensure that students who you know will benefit the most have the tool in sight.

4. If you have a student who seems to become agitated by the visual timer or seems to obsess over watching the time, use this as an opportunity for a private discussion. You might want to explore what the student's concern is so that you can best support them. For instance, you may explore:

   • Is the student concerned about running out of time?
   • Is the student focusing on others' progress rather than his or her own?
   • Would the student prefer another type of device to serve as a reminder?

The Premack Principle

The Premack Principle (also known as Grandma's Rule) is a psychological theory that proposes the following: A person is more willing to do a less desirable activity *first* in order to get to do a more desirable activity *later*. The Premack Principle is evident in the commonly used adage, "First eat your dinner, and then you can have dessert." While this theory has been demonstrated in practice, have you noticed that it does not seem to always apply to some students? Why? **Because kids with ADHD often have difficulty delaying gratification.** It's hard to imagine the future becoming the present when their sense of time is "now" and "not now." Children with ADHD are focused on the negative feelings of what they must do in the present moment—as opposed to the feelings they will have in future once that task is complete.

Asking students the following questions can help them create an image in their mind of what it will feel like to be done with a difficult or challenging assignment, and what they can look forward to as a result of having finished.

- How do you think you will feel once you are done? Relieved? Proud? Relaxed?
- What will you be able to do as a result of finishing? Move on to a more interesting activity? Get a "completion" on the assignment? Acquire knowledge that will be helpful?

Even with the best of intentions, it is still sometimes challenging to help students face the work that they need to do, especially if an assignment is challenging in such a way that it makes them feel badly about themselves. Sometimes, people try to brush over the difficulty that a student might be having by encouraging him or her to "go on." They might try providing words of encouragement by stating, "Come on, you got this. Piece of cake." However, this approach may feel invalidating to some, and they may even feel that the person making these statements really doesn't understand them. Sometimes, the greatest support that you can provide a child who is struggling is honest empathy and compassion: "I know that doing this work is really hard and frustrating. I am here if you need my support or help."

WHAT ELSE CAN BE PART OF ADHD?

In the next chapter, we will introduce the concept of executive function and describe how that impacts learning, motivation, and behavior. As you will see, gaining a greater understanding of the executive functions is vital for anyone who works with children, either professionally or personally. However, for those of you who *specifically* work with students with ADHD, a crucial fact cannot be overlooked: **ADHD is an executive function challenge.** A person cannot have ADHD without having at least some challenges in executive functioning. There is tremendous overlap between the two constructs, both in terms of symptoms and their real-life impact.

On the other hand, it is also important to keep in mind that someone *can* have executive functioning deficits without having ADHD. However, unlike ADHD—which is a formal diagnosis in the *DSM*—a person cannot be *diagnosed* with executive function deficits; rather, it is more of a description at this time. The fact that the *DSM* does not have a diagnostic category related to the executive functions has some significant implications when it comes to students who experience challenges in these areas. In particular, while most professionals in the field agree on *what* the executive functions are, we still have different ways of describing them. In addition, because there is no official diagnostic procedure, students are often not appropriately assessed and, in turn, often don't receive the appropriate accommodations, modifications, and support.

A few other issues are important to mention that can be part of having ADHD or may be highly correlated.

- **Learning disabilities** – 31% to 45% of children with ADHD have a learning disability, and a significant number of those with learning challenges have dyslexia (DuPaul, et al, 2012). We find this is a very important statistic to take note of. Very often, especially while they are young, students may be red flagged because of their lack of focus and behavior. However, there are times when the lack of focus and challenging behavior is caused by the child's reaction to the difficulty he or she is experiencing in learning the expected material. In addition, many students who have ADHD are highly intelligent and can compensate for learning challenges early on until the expectations exceed their ability to mask their difficulties. We encourage educators and parents to make sure that students who are suspected of having ADHD are also assessed for their learning profile as well.

- **Sleep disruption** – Most studies find that between 33% to 50% of people with ADHD experience difficulty falling asleep and/or staying asleep in an appropriate amount of time. This situation can create tremendous challenges for both parents and students, and can have a significant impact on learning and behavior. In recognizing that sleep issues are a byproduct of ADHD and not necessarily due to lack of effort by a parent or student, it may be reasonable in some cases to accommodate scheduling concerns on IEP or 504 Plans.

- **Depression** – 17% of children with ADHD experience depression (National Survey of Children's Health, 2016). It is not always clear whether the depression has a clinical basis or whether it arises because students sometimes unintentionally experience such a mismatch between their environments and expectations.

- **Behavior or conduct problem** – 52% of children with ADHD exhibit behavioral challenges (National Survey of Children's Health, 2016). It's important to keep in mind that just as with depression, the challenging behavior may develop as a result of students feeling misunderstood or that expectations are unreasonable even when they see others around them managing fine. We firmly believe that every parent who has a child diagnosed with ADHD must receive parent coaching, just as educators must receive proper training to work with them in the classroom.

- **Anxiety** – 33% of children with ADHD struggle with anxiety (National Survey of Children's Health, 2016). We call this the "hidden disability" because we think that anxiety is almost always in the room with these students. Often what we witness as poor behavior is driven by their anxiety.

- **Cognitive hyperactivity** – While your student may be looking directly at you, he or she may be having a bombardment of thoughts, or may be hyper-focused on some internal activity.

- **Difficulty learning from past experiences** – Time is "now" and "not now." That was "then."

- **Difficulty transitioning from one thought or activity to another** – Remember, ADHD is a challenge of attention regulation, not just focus.

- **Difficulty taking another person's perspective** – It's not that they don't care about those around them, it's often just that there is so much internal chaos to sort out that they haven't gotten to thinking about the other person *yet*.

- **Sloppy handwriting** – Have you ever noticed the difference in a student's handwriting when he or she is on stimulant medication vs. when he or she is not—it may seem completely different. So, it is not always *learning* how to print. Instead, it may be about doing it correctly with everything else going on, both internally and externally.

- **Difficulty with written expression** – Between the bombardment of thoughts that may occur, and the challenges in regulating their focus and getting organized, plus the challenges in executive function skills, writing an essay from start to finish may be especially challenging for those with ADHD. We will provide support for written expression in the next chapter.

- **Difficulty delaying gratification** – It's hard to imagine the future becoming the present when time is "now" and "not now."

- **Difficulty tolerating boredom** – After even the most exciting events, once it's over, it's over—now what are we doing? Remember, they have below normal levels of neurotransmitters when they are not stimulated.

Beware of the quiet child… you don't have to be hyperactive to have ADHD and its related impairments. Even if children are compliant, it does not mean that their neurobiology is not impacting them.

2.
What Are Executive Functions?

WHAT WE KNOW ABOUT EXECUTIVE FUNCTIONS

The executive functions refer to a set of metacognitive processes that govern our ability to plan ahead, solve problems, pay attention, control our impulses, manage our time, and engage in goal-oriented behavior. Broadly speaking, the executive functions govern how efficiently we do whatever it is that we decide to do. Therefore, they are often collectively referred to as the CEO (Chief Executive Officer) of the brain because they comprise its mental control center.

Until the current decade, there was not much talk in classrooms or amongst parents about the concept of "executive functions." That lack of understanding was problematic, given that they play such a central role in helping us understand and support student learning, performance, and behavior. Although our knowledge regarding the executive functions has increased, there is still a considerable lack of understanding regarding *how* the executive functions develop and *how* they impact learning, motivation, and behavior. In fact, this chapter could also be titled "What *Is* Executive Function?" since there is still not a universal agreement on how we discuss this part of our brain's operation.

The executive functions are located primarily in the prefrontal cortex, which is the front part of the brain, right behind the forehead. The prefrontal cortex is the last part of the brain to develop, which means that our ability to plan, make decisions, and regulate our behavior is compromised until our brains are fully developed (and this does not happen until about 25 years of age!). This is a startling fact when you consider all of the major life decisions that we are often expected to make in our 20s.

In the next section, we'll look at each of the executive functions. Keep in mind that unlike ADHD an individual cannot be diagnosed with Executive Function Disorder or executive function deficits. These are descriptive terms; however, the *DSM*, which contains descriptions, symptoms, and other criteria for diagnosing mental disorders, does not have a diagnostic category for executive function. Therefore, while most professionals in the field agree on what the executive functions are, we still have different ways of describing them. We include seven executive function categories based on Brown's (2005) model:

- Initiation and activation
- Sustaining and shifting focus
- Planning and organizing
- Regulating alertness, sustaining effort, and processing speed
- Working memory
- Self-monitoring
- Emotion regulation

A diagram summarizing each of these categories—and their overall role as the CEO of the brain—can be found on the next page.

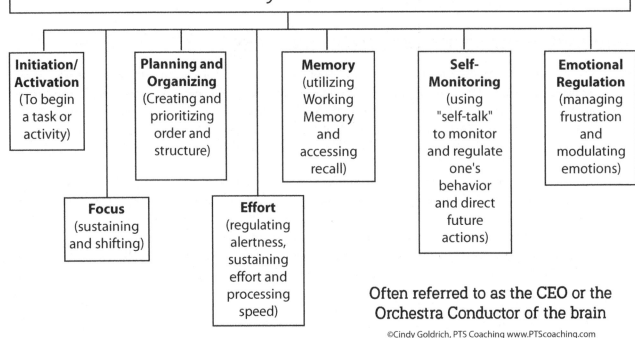

But here is another significant fact to consider: The prefrontal cortex is thinner in people with ADHD, and it matures more slowly. Some people take longer than others to develop their executive functions. For those with ADHD, there can be a delay of three to six years in the development of the prefrontal cortex and associated executive function skills. That delay has nothing to do with intelligence (Brown, 2005).

In this chapter, we explore the difference between executive functioning and intelligence, and we'll also talk about what you can do if you are concerned that a student may have executive function challenges. Then, we will explore how each executive function impacts students—as well as adults—and provide some activities to help improve executive function.

One final consideration as you read through this chapter: You will often hear these executive functions referred to as executive function *skills*. The word *skills* is vital to recognize in this context. Whenever a person has a skill deficit, such as a student with dyslexia who struggles to learn to read, we recognize that this person needs additional education, support, and, sometimes, accommodations and modifications. We don't simply say, "Well, we taught you how to decode words, so now you need just to work harder." The same perspective is important when addressing students who are struggling with regard to one of the executive function areas. Therefore, when Jonny—yet again—fails to unpack his backpack at the beginning of the school day, rather than becoming frustrated and reprimanding Jonny, we need to realize that "getting started" is a *skill* in which Jonny is lagging, and we need to teach and support him in developing that skill.

INTELLIGENCE AND EXECUTIVE FUNCTIONING

Although the executive functions serve as the mental control center of the brain, executive functioning is a construct that is separate from intelligence. Therefore, a person can have an extremely high IQ but have very weak executive functions. This fact explains why there is often a discrepancy between IQ and achievement. Students may be very bright, yet be chronic underachievers. It also explains why a student who seemed to know the test material might have ended up doing very poorly on the test itself. When this happens, teachers and parents often make assumptions that the student didn't study or didn't try. However, it is possible that the student's executive function challenges got in the way. For example, he or she may not have been able to access working memory, process information quickly enough, or stay focused on the problems at hand. This is why we often say that **ADHD is not a problem of knowing what to do; rather, it's a problem of doing what you know**. Indeed, studies have shown that strategy, or how you do what you do, contributes between 15% and 25% of performance on measures of intelligence, achievement, and neuropsychological abilities. Behaviors related to planning, flexibility, and self-monitoring are consistently the most powerful strategic behaviors correlating with better performance (Naglieri & Goldstein, 2014).

Keep in mind that it is also possible for a student to have a very high IQ and still be performing well academically inspite of having weak executive function skills. However, at some point, that student may no longer be able to compensate for his or her weaker executive function skills. It's not unusual to get calls from parents who are perplexed and concerned because their child—who did fine in grade school and got into a wonderful college—has now been put on academic suspension during the first semester of college. We believe this dynamic happens because, during grade school, the student had the necessary supports (both at home and at school) that allowed him or her to focus on academic performance. For example, the parents may be helping manage all of the typical responsibilities, such as laundry and meal preparation, and may place certain restrictions on socializing. The teachers often provide regular homework, quizzes, and tests throughout the semester, whereas in college, generally there is only a mid-term and a final. And parents don't have the benefit of quarterly reports and teacher conferences. Without the same support systems to fall back on, many students (and parents), are caught off guard until it is too late to make adjustments.

A. INITIATION AND ACTIVATION

Initiation and activation are the skills needed to get started on a task. Whether it's getting started with a routine task, such as unpacking a backpack, or a more difficult task, such as beginning a book report, some students struggle and may give the appearance of being lazy, unmotivated, resistant, or just plain procrastinating. However, when we dig a little deeper, we may find that these students have difficulty getting started because they simply don't know how or where to begin. Remember that students with ADHD also have a much harder time activating their brain when they are not intrinsically interested or motivated by the task at hand.

In addition, transitions can be especially challenging for students with ADHD and executive functioning challenges. When we ask students to transition from one activity to another, we are actually asking them to do three separate and often individually challenging, steps: (1) stop the activity, (2) move to the next activity, and (3) start the new activity. Transitions can be supported more fully when we break the movement into three parts and address each step separately. As always, each student and each class of students is different, so don't give up when one strategy doesn't seem to work. An approach that worked for one group of students will not necessarily work for the next. It's possible that a slight change is all you need to help the transition go more smoothly. In the next section, we discuss the three components of the transition process and present strategies that can help make your students more successful in transitioning from one task to the next.

Step 1: Stop the Activity

Imagine that your students are engaged in a writing task and working well, but you see that it's almost time for math instruction. It took some of your students so long to get started, but they got through it. You supported them in working through those initial challenges, and now you have to stop them. Often, it feels as painful for you as it will for the student, but there are ways to make this go well for everyone. First, **evaluate the problem** by finding out what the student's connection is to the current activity. This is an important step before you can help him or her disengage from that activity. Second, **explore options for stopping** that help your students start the transition process more smoothly and more easily. The following are some considerations to help you through these two processes:

Evaluate the Problem:

1. Consider what types of activities or what time of day your student has a difficult time stopping what he or she is doing. You may notice that there are predictable times or situations where stopping is most challenging. Write down and track these times and activities.

2. Through your observation and questioning of these times and situations, see if you can learn the following:

   - Is the student happily engaged in the activity, perhaps making it harder to stop?

   - Is the student hyper-focused on the activity? This can make it challenging to notice the passage of time or the expectations of others.

   - Is the student concerned about what will happen if he or she needs to stop before the activity has been completed? Is the student:

      - Worried about how he or she will be graded?

      - Worried that he or she won't have another opportunity to complete the task?

      - Disappointed because he or she is enjoying the activity and wants to see it to its conclusion?

Explore Options for Stopping:

1. **Set Expectations**: Discuss the specific expectation for stopping at the beginning of the activity. Let the students know how much time they will have and what they will be doing once the activity is over.

2. **Use Visual Timers:** Whether or not your students can tell time yet, the use of a visual timer allows them to see the passage of time and how much time is left for an activity. Try getting in the habit of setting a timer for each time of day between transitions. Watching the passage of time helps students build their time management skills and allows them to gain an understanding of what a unit of time really means. Visual timers also allow you to designate a third party to say, "The timer says it's time to stop now." You can't blame the person! You will be surprised how quickly your students will start asking you to set the timer once this routine is built.

3. **Plan a Warning:** A simple strategy to build into your routine is giving students a warning before a task is about to be over. The amount of time you give your students will depend on the activity and the needs of the students, but a five-minute warning is typically appropriate. Providing students with this warning will help them anticipate the end of the task.

4. **Acknowledge What You See**: Sometimes, students can be so hyper-focused on what they are doing that it's more challenging to pull them away. A simple comment of recognition can create connection and help the student stay calm and reflective. For example, "Jessie, I see that you are working on the third problem. Please prepare to stop in a few minutes."

5. **Help Plan the Stopping Point:** Some students have a hard time figuring out a good stopping point, so they try to work to completion, either rushing or not ending when needed. If needed, speak directly with the student to help him or her plan a good stopping point, as well as a plan for when the student can re-engage with the work. For example, you can ask, "What part do you think is reasonable to finish in the five minutes that are left?" Students who are still reluctant to stop the activity may need your help in developing this plan so they can learn how to do so more independently in the future.

6. **Use a Transition Coach:** A transition coach can either be the teacher, the aide, or perhaps a student in the class who will help signal when it is time to stop, move, or start an activity. **More detail regarding the use of a transition coach is provided on the following page.**

Stopping: Help from the Transition Coach

. . .

Do you ever notice that after awhile, a teacher's voice may sound like the Charlie Brown character—"Wa, wa, wa"? Students may see your lips moving, but they are not focusing on the words you are saying. When this occurs, it can be frustrating and exhausting to tell your students, "Okay everyone, it's time to…" or "Come on, we need to…" over and over again. In these cases, it helps to have a transition coach. The following are some strategies that you can try with your students:

- Use some type of external signal when it is time to stop an activity. A gentle bell, a meditation chime, or a small harp can be played to let everyone know that it's time to stop, return to their seats, and be quiet. You can set up a warning sound and a final sound to mark the expectations.

- Give students the opportunity to be the transition coach. Let the student know in advance that he or she will be in charge of letting others know when it is time to stop an activity. This technique is especially helpful for supporting students who have the hardest time stopping. By putting that student in charge of making the sound, he or she is more likely to lead by example and do as expected. By talking with the student in advance, you also help raise his or her awareness of what it takes to prepare to stop.

- Consider how much time you think the class will need in order to comfortably stop the activity.

- Plan in advance for how you will deal with any stragglers. This is especially important if one of your students will be assisting you in managing the transition.

Step 2: Move to the Next Activity

All the students have finally concluded their writing assignment, but now they really need to get started on math. You've asked your students to move to their math groups, grab the correct notebook and writing utensil, and turn to today's page in the textbook. Should be simple, right? Come on, you've been doing this since September! Yet, somehow, you have those same students who are sitting in the correct seat but don't have any of the materials that you asked them to get out. Sound familiar? This will be difficult for some students because they may have missed pieces of what you said, can't find some of the materials you asked them to use, or simply got distracted by a more interesting activity.

As we have learned, getting started is one executive function skill that is challenging for individuals with ADHD and executive dysfunction. While getting started comes naturally to some students, others need our help before they can be successful on their own. **The following worksheet can be a great tool to help students who need some extra support getting started.** Some students will benefit a lot from having these three prompts—and, hopefully, it will take the burden off of you as the teacher! After using these prompts over and over again, students will start to learn what they need to do to get started without needing extra support.

The first thing that students should think about before starting a task is what materials they need to perform the task. Next, they should ask themselves what their body should look like while performing the activity. This might include a consideration of where they are sitting and whether or not they are being appropriate. The last part involves asking the teacher any questions that they may have about the assignment. Oftentimes, we find that students are sitting and just not starting on their work. While it may appear as if they are being lazy or refusing to work, it is also likely that they aren't exactly sure what it is that they're supposed to be doing.

Some students will benefit from having a visual representation of the worksheet, while other students may not need this support. For students who would benefit from a visual aid, try laminating the worksheet near the student's workspace as a frequent reference. You or your student can use a dry erase marker to answer the three questions. As always, consider your individual students and support them as needed.

Getting Ready to Get Started

. . .

The purpose of this worksheet is to help you get focused as you begin a new activity. You may find it helpful to have this on your desk as a reminder, or write on it for practice.

Instructions:

Think about what activity or assignment you are being asked to do, and work to answer these three questions about the activity.

1. **What material do I need?** Take a moment to think about any materials that you would need to be successful with the assignment, and make sure you have them with you. If you need any materials that you don't have, or are not sure where they are, make sure to ask for help to get these before you move on.	**What materials do I need?**
2. **What should my body look like?** Consider where you should be sitting, and how you should be sitting to be able to do your best work.	**What should my body look like?**
3. **What questions do I have?** Is there anything you still need to find out before you can actually start the task? If so, ask the teacher or a friend so that you are now ready to get started.	**What questions do I have?**

Step 3: Start the New Activity

For many children (and adults!), starting a new activity is about feeling ready to begin, both emotionally and physically. We need to teach the skills to start, just as we would teach our students the steps involved in completing a math problem. The following are some strategies that will help your students emotionally and physically prepare to start an assignment. While having this discussion with your students in advance of an assignment may seem laborious, we find that the upfront investment in time dramatically shortens the time that we spend redirecting and managing the additional fallout from the work not done.

Emotional Preparation:

☐ Discuss the potential benefits of getting started easier and sooner.

- They have to do the work anyway, so stalling and postponing doesn't make it go away.

- Getting started quickly means less wasted time and, in turn, more free time.

- Being able to work independently means less arguing and more freedom from adults.

☐ If the student is still stuck, explore what else might be getting in the way of getting started.

- Are the expectations reasonable?

- Is the amount of time allotted for the activity reasonable?

- How is their emotional fuel tank? Do they need a break, a snack, or a stress release?

- Has procrastination been "effective" in the past?

☐ How's their mindset?[1]

- Do they feel confident that they have the materials and information they need?

- Do they understand the expectations?

- Do they have the ability to complete the work or access to the help they will need?

Physical Preparation:

☐ Location: Consider how much supervision or assistance the students will require.

☐ Seating: Be willing to be flexible and creative. Examine different seating options that work for that student. You can refer to the section "Let Them Move" in Chapter 1 for more details. The following are some options to consider:

- Standing desk

- Lap desk

- "Husband Pillow" (backrest pillow with arms)

- Ball chair

- Rug

☐ The visual space:

- Clear of excess clutter or unnecessary distractions

- Display a motivating statement, picture, or drawing that may help motivate the student to stay on task. For example, "When I stay on task I get things done and I am happier," or perhaps an image that the student finds calming or inspiring.

---

1 See Chapter 6 for more details about mindset

☐ Supplies:
- Bulletin board
- Folder caddy
- Two dry erase boards or scratch pads
- Movable supply caddy (and a closet full of extra supplies)
- Visual timer
- Water? Snacks? Music? Fidgets?

How Do You Start Your Engine?

When you want to drive your car, a variety of steps you take to get it into motion. You unlock your car, buckle your seatbelt, put the key in the ignition, and turn it until the motor engages to start the engine. Similarly, before students can get to work in the classroom, they need to get their engines started too.

Consider your own routines as you get ready to start working on a project. These are often the habits that you do subconsciously in order to prime your body to work. For example, as a teacher getting ready to lesson plan for the week, you might gather your curriculum materials, your lesson planner, and any pens you like to use, and find a space where you can easily lay everything out. You might start by cross-checking calendars for any special events that would change your planning and anything else you need to get you the right information for the week ahead. You're probably not consciously deciding to do each small step, but by getting into the practice of planning time after time, you know the routines that work well for you and you'll often find yourself just doing them.

However, students who have a hard time getting started need help developing these positive habits. Although we have looked at some tools to help kids get started *in the classroom*, there are other times when they need more of a system to help them get working—namely, when they must complete assignments *at home*. We want our students to be successful with the work that we send home with them at night, but we know that after a long day of school, this can be challenging for a variety of reasons. Students are often exhausted at the end of the day, and motivating themselves to do more work can take extra effort. For some students, without the supports of teachers and materials at school, they may struggle to know where to begin and finding a space where they can be successful. Many students are actually working so very hard at school to hold it all together and be trying their best that they get home and are fairly emotionally drained.

The following worksheet is a tool that can be used with students to help them build a routine at home that allows them to be successful when it comes to getting started on their homework assignments.

How Do You Start Your Engine?

· · ·

When we are at school, we often have good routines for getting started on assignments, and our teacher is there to help us when we need it. However, at home, it can sometimes be more challenging to limit distractions and create an environment where you are ready to do your best work. This tool can be used to help you get the distractions out of the way and create the space that you need to be successful.

Instructions:

1. The three sections on this tool ask you to think about what you do when you get home from school before you are ready to start your homework. Everyone has slightly different routines, so think about a routine that allows you to get ready to work.

2. In each section, write down the first, next, then last thing that you do before you can focus on your work. Make sure that by the time you have finished the last part, you have distractions out of the way and are ready to go.

Example:

First, I will…	Next, I will…	Last, I will…	
Walk my dog	Have a snack	Check my emails	**Now I am ready to work.**

Now you try!

First, I will…	Next, I will…	Last, I will…	
			Now I am ready to work.

Planning for Schedule Changes

Some students just do better when they know what to expect—regardless of whether or not they are diagnosed with ADHD. Preparation, guidance, and connection are the keys to easing transitions. Although posting a weekly schedule is always a good idea, the reality is that there are times—both planned and otherwise—when that schedule needs to be adjusted, either temporarily or permanently. Challenges arise when this change creates significant stress or disappointment for one or several students. Sometimes, adults postpone or avoid sharing information that may be upsetting to others, hoping that with less time to protest, students will "go with the flow." **However, it is important to let your class know of an impending change as early as possible for a few reasons:**

- We all do better when we feel that we have choices and a degree of input or control. Having accurate information about the upcoming change gives students an opportunity to modify or alter their plans.

- Emotion regulation for some students requires greater awareness, support, and opportunity to practice. We want to give students ample occasions to learn to manage their frustration and adjust their responses, as well as to support them when the change is more than they can typically manage.

- It is far easier to deal with a meltdown or problem when there is still time *before* the event. In contrast, it is much more difficult to manage a student's reaction while simultaneously helping everyone else get to where they need to go or do what they need to do.

Here are a few tips that can benefit the entire class when a schedule change occurs:

1. If there is a particular activity that you know a student looks forward to that needs to be changed or canceled (e.g., an assembly, gym class, etc.), when possible, tell that student individually ahead of the class. Doing so will allow you to connect empathetically with the student (e.g., "I am sorry, I know you really enjoy…" or "I know you might be disappointed that…") and give the student an opportunity to react more discreetly. If possible, you might also be able to discuss alternative plans or options.

2. When appropriate, ask the class how they will manage the change. For instance, if something is canceled, ask your students how they can best take advantage of the "gift of time." This can also be a great opportunity to discuss the concept of positive reflection and have students focus on the upside of the change (e.g., "And this is good because…").

3. If the change involves missing out on an opportunity that the students were looking forward to, discuss any plans that are being considered to reschedule the event. If possible, put these plans into writing so students can be reminded of when they can look forward to the event. If the event cannot be rescheduled, discuss any alternate ways that students can perhaps get a similar experience. Again, we want to help students learn to deal with frustration, not to just help them avoid it.

#2: SUSTAINING AND SHIFTING FOCUS

These are the skills related to controlling who and what you are paying attention to, staying on topic, filtering out other thoughts and ideas, and moving on from one activity to another as is appropriate. The ability to focus can be quite challenging for people with ADHD, especially if they are not intrinsically motivated or genuinely interested in the task at hand. In addition, even when they can focus, they may be easily distracted by external stimuli or internal thoughts. They genuinely have a more difficult time screening out distractions that interrupt their focus. And as we discussed in Chapter 1, they may have significant trouble shifting their attention when they *can* focus, perhaps because they have become so hyper-focused on a particular thought or task.

Mindfulness

The practice of mindfulness involves learning to be present in the moment with a calming and accepting attitude. Mindfulness can help all students in promoting happiness and relieving stress. For students with ADHD, research shows that mindfulness practices can have a lot of benefits for sustaining focus and reducing anxiety. There are many great mindfulness resources available, including *Mindful Learning* by Drs. Craig Hassed and Dr. Richard Chambers. Hassed and Chambers discuss the benefits of mindfulness for all individuals and go through techniques that parents and educators can use to support students. **The following worksheet and handout share a couple of tools you can use with your students to practice mindfulness.**

Mindful Mazes

Mindful mazes are a strategy to help students get back on track after a moment of distraction or frustration. The idea with these mazes is that they give students something to focus their attention on for a short amount of time. In doing so, students are then able to regain a state of mindfulness and bring this state of mind back to their learning. Use mindful mazes with students in times when they need to refocus. Students can use their eyes to track through the maze, or a finger to get through.

The following are two mindful mazes can be given to students to help them refocus their attention.

Mindful Mazes

...

Mindful Mazes

· · ·

S.T.O.P.

• • •

The "S.T.O.P" acronym is one technique that can be used to help students pause in a moment of stress or anxiety and regain mindfulness to get back on track. This strategy asks students to pause whatever it is that they are doing, breathe, and notice what is happening in their body and surroundings before deciding if they should proceed, or if it's better not to.

Stop: Stop what you are doing and pause momentarily, wherever you are and whatever you are doing.

Take a breath: Take a moment to breathe and reconnect with your breath. Let your breathing be slow and steady.

Observe: Notice what is going on around you and within your body. What is your mind focusing on? What does your body feel like? What are you doing?

Proceed: Get back to what you were doing, or use what you have noticed to decide to stop. You might need to seek out other strategies, take a break from what you were doing, or stop a task that was distracting you from what you should be doing.

S: Stop.

T: Take a breath.

O: Observe.

P: Proceed (or don't).

The Pomodoro Technique

The Pomodoro Technique, developed by Francesco Cirillo in the 1980s, is a time management strategy that helps increase focus and attention. When Francesco was a college student, he noticed that he was unable to work productively and that his friends were completing the same amount of work in less time. As he examined how he worked, he decided to challenge himself to see if he could work for 10 minutes straight and be *really* productive during this time. He used his kitchen timer that was shaped like a "pomodoro," which is the Italian word for "tomato."

At first, he struggled to concentrate well for that long, but as he began to plan out his work—along with scheduled break times that he could count on—he found that he became much more productive. Now, business executives and students around the world use his Pomodoro Technique. In fact, his technique is so popular that several apps have been developed based on this method.

At its core, the Pomodoro Technique involves breaking down work into manageable intervals, with small, scheduled breaks in between. A "pomodoro" is a unit of time that you intend to work on a specific task without stopping (e.g., 15 minutes). It is the time that you are committing to stay focused on the work you are doing. By setting your intention to work *uninterrupted* on a specific task for 10 to 20 minutes—with a planned break to follow—most people report that they can concentrate deeper and work more effectively. This, in turn, reduces the overall time that you need to spend completing your work. **The following handout describes some basics of the Pomodoro Technique, followed by a planner that students can use to track their pomodoros.**

The Pomodoro Technique

• • •

- List the tasks that you need to complete on the Pomodoro Planner (p. 31) in the order in which you plan to complete them. Each line on the planner represents one pomodoro (e.g., 15 minutes). If a task will take longer than one pomodoro, list it on multiple lines.

- On your planner, include any other obligations you have that will take away from your free time (e.g., packing for a hockey game, chores, etc.).

- The last task should include putting away your materials, so that you are ready for the next activity and will get credit for the work you accomplished.

- If you notice a distracting thought while you are working on a pomodoro (e.g., "I need to tell Josh something"), try to resist the urge to act on the thought. Instead, notice the thought and let it go. If you need to, "park" that thought by writing it down and commit to act on it during either your break or when you are finished with all your work. The more you stay focused on the task at hand, the more effective and efficient you will be in completing your work. **Protect the pomodoro!**

- Plan to take a five-minute **timed** break after each pomodoro. Every few breaks, make sure to include an energizing break (e.g., get up and walk around) to keep your body alert.

- After three pomodoros, take a 20- to 30-minute **timed** break. The better you become at disciplining yourself to respect the timer, the more quickly and efficiently you will complete your work so you can enjoy your free time.

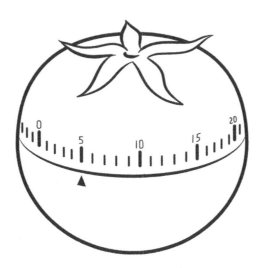

The Pomodoro Technique has many beneficial uses in the classroom. **The following activity will help you teach your students how to use this strategy for focusing in the classroom.** The goal is that after you do this activity, your students will be ready to effectively and independently use the Pomodoro Technique in the classroom when they are guided to. **On the next page, you will find the Pomodoro Planner, which you can use along with this technique in your classroom.**

1. Depending on the students' grade level, you may want to start with some brief history of the Pomodoro Technique, as we previously described.

2. Explain to students how the technique works:
   - *We use the Pomodoro Technique to help us work at our highest level of productivity.*
   - *During a pomodoro, the goal is that all of your focus is on the task, and anything that pops in your head or tries to distract you during this time should be pushed aside. It has to be saved for when the pomodoro is over.*
   - *Once the pomodoro ends, you get to take a short break from your work. This is also very important because it allows your brain to reset. When you give your brain a chance to reset, you can stay at your highest level of productivity for a much longer period of time than if you just tried to keep going. Your break might be reading a book, getting up to go to the bathroom or for a drink of water, or taking care of something that wanted to distract you during your pomodoro.*
   - *When the break time is over, the pomodoro starts again, and we get back to work.*

3. You may want to give students a small sticky note or notepad on their desk where they can jot down any thoughts or distractions that try to make their way into the pomodoro. This can be a helpful tool to help them keep going through the pomodoro.

4. Introduce the activity.
   - Pick an appropriate activity for your students that will realistically take them at least 30 minutes to complete. This longer length of time will allow them to get into the routine of a pomodoro. Most writing tasks are a good option for this activity.

5. Have students clear their work space of anything that might distract them from the current task.

6. Set a timer for 15 minutes and explain to students that they are now in the first pomodoro. Remind them to put any distractions aside for this short time and that they will get to take a break soon from their hard work.

7. Once the timer goes off, instruct students to take a break. It is very important to the Pomodoro Technique that they actually take a break from work. You can set the timer again for 3-5 minutes to structure a short break.

8. Repeat the pomodoro!!

Instructions:

To use the Pomodoro Planner, start by choosing a short increment of time during which you want students to be actively working (e.g., 10, 15, 20 minutes). Look at the assignments and responsibilities that you need students to complete in a given amount of time. Write these tasks down in the order that you intend students to complete them. If you anticipate that students will need more than one pomodoro for a task, then write the task on multiple lines. Have students record how long each task actually took them to help them become aware of the passage of time.

The Pomodoro Planner

• • •

Task to Complete	Check off when complete	Was the work put where it needs to go?	How long did it take?

To Do Later—Protect the Pomodoro!

#3: PLANNING AND ORGANIZING

Planning is the ability to anticipate future events. It involves setting a goal and creating a strategy to meet that goal. Planning for a future event—whether it involves arriving somewhere on time or completing an assignment by its due date—requires forethought, estimation, and problem solving. It requires the ability to identify and organize what materials are needed, to prioritize which tasks need to be completed first, and to determine the sequence in which tasks need to be completed.

For students with ADHD, planning and organizing can be especially difficult. Because key aspects of the reward system are underactive in their brains, they are focused on what they want to do right now instead of what they need to do in the future. Remember, time for them is "now" and "not now." They have trouble dealing with the delayed gratification that future rewards offer. In addition, as we mentioned, their internal clocks are often not as accurate as that of other individuals, and they don't necessarily think through the details involved in a given task and how long each task might take.

Passage of Time

How often do you tell your students something to the effect of, "You have 20 minutes to do this activity"? In most cases, your students don't even take a moment to look at the current time when you spoke! In addition, how often do you find that when time is up, some of your students are still in the middle of the activity and very frustrated that you're suddenly telling them that they have to stop? In order to help individuals with ADHD become more skilled at planning, we need to help them "see" the future. This process involves providing them with initial external support and immediate feedback, and then gradually shifting to providing them with more delayed feedback that teaches them to utilize their internal controls. When we set time expectations for our students, we are often trying to guide the amount of effort and substance that they put into an activity, or trying to give them an awareness of when it's time to move on. However, it doesn't always seem to mean very much when that time is up and the students are simply not ready to be done.

What does 20 minutes really mean? Well, it depends on the student and his or her executive functioning abilities. Remember: The ability to plan ahead and manage time is one of our executive functioning skills. However, children with executive function challenges often have a difficult time understanding the passage of time and, in turn, struggle to appropriately plan for future events. So, what does saying, "You have 20 minutes" mean to a student who deals with these challenges? Well… not very much.

However, just as we can directly teach many of the other executive function skills, we can also teach students to understand the passage of time. **The following two activities can be used with your students to help them gain some awareness of what time really feels like as it goes by.**

Passage of Time

• • •

For this exercise, ask students to complete a drawing activity while they simultaneously estimate when a certain amount of time (e.g., 10 minutes) has passed. The purpose of this activity is to get students into the habit of more accurately estimating when time has passed (as opposed to completing the actual drawing itself).

Materials:

- White paper or construction paper
- Darker paper to cover up classroom clocks
- Markers

Instructions:

1. Start by explaining that for this activity they will be drawing a picture of what they imagine their life will look like in five years.

2. Tell your students that they will have 10 minutes to complete this activity. Emphasize that the purpose of the activity is to decide *when* the 10 minutes have passed—more so than completing the activity itself.

3. When students think that 10 minutes have gone by, they should put their markers down, wherever they are in their drawing. This is how they will express when they think that 10 minutes have passed.

4. Whenever a student signals that he or she thinks time is up, mark down the time that the student stopped.

5. Allow students about 15 to 20 minutes for this activity in order to give them room to overestimate the passage of time (or stop the activity beforehand if all the students have already stopped drawing).

6. When you end the activity, explain to students how much time has actually passed. Share some of the most common stopping points and the amount of time that had actually gone by at these points.

Let's Go on a Field Trip

...

Time awareness plays an integral role in preparation and performance. Bringing it to the foreground helps everyone be more responsible and accountable. And what better way to help your students learn about their sense of the passage of time than to test it out? As a bonus, they will be more mindful and cooperative when it comes to being places on time.

Choose a few places around the school that the students need to visit regularly:

- the gym
- the cafeteria
- the music room
- the nurse's office
- the main office
- the auditorium

Then, choose a few activities that the students are routinely responsible for doing. For example:

- Coming into the class, unpacking their backpack, and preparing to work
- Packing up at the end of the day, including deciding what needs to come home and packing it accordingly

Ask the students to predict as precisely as possible how long traveling to each place or preparing for each task will take. Then, using a timer, ask students to see how long each task actually takes. You may want students to repeat each task a few times to get an average.

After the students complete the exercise, use the following questions to guide a class discussion that has them reflect on their experience:

1. How accurately did you predict the passage of time?

2. Did you feel you were going faster or slower while you were focused on how long it would take?

3. Now that you know how long each task actually takes, what will you do to adjust your schedule in preparation?

4. How can you best support yourself in being timely for your events and tasks?

Creating a Productive Workspace

"Outer order contributes to inner calm" (Rubin, 2018 p. 297). As teachers, we try to create classroom environments that are organized and create a calming atmosphere. For example, we might direct students as to what color folder to put a certain worksheet in, and frequently work to minimize clutter around students' workspaces. However, we eventually want our students to create this environment for themselves and on their own. We want them to be able to develop a space where they can be successful, have their materials organized, and have an environment where they can focus at their full potential.

In order to help our students be productive in their work environment, we can teach them to create a workspace that will help them be successful learners. **The following worksheet is intended to help students think about what type of workspace will keep them organized and make them into more productive learners.** Start this activity by guiding a conversation about the various characteristics that students should consider with regard to their work environment. For example, their workspace should be clean and organized, there should be helpful tools around for completing the work, and there should be enough physical space to do the work. After having this discussion, ask the students to draw a picture of what their ideal workspace would look like. Then, have them answer a few questions about why they chose the space they did.

Creating a Productive Workspace

• • •

Instructions:

In the box below, draw a picture of what your ideal workspace would look like. What type of workspace will allow you to be as productive as possible?

What types of tools did you put in your workspace?

_____

_____

What did you choose to leave out of your workspace? Why?

_____

_____

How will the workspace you created help you to be a productive learner?

_____

_____

Locker Organization

Typically speaking, when children move on from elementary school to middle school, they make the transition from using a desk or classroom cubby system to using a personal locker in the hallway. As part of this transition, students go from having their personal things inside the classroom (where they are for most of their day, with the assistance of their teacher beside them to help them stay organized) to being completely on their own. Many students are ready for this type of independence, but for others, this responsibility can create challenges. In particular, students who have executive functioning challenges with planning and organization may not be as ready developmentally to make this transition. Therefore, they will often still require additional supports to be successful with this new responsibility.

When students move on to middle school, as teachers, we can no longer personally manage their organization. However, we can give them tools to be more successful on their own. **The following worksheet is intended to guide students through thinking about what is important in organizing their locker.** Answering these questions will help your students visualize their locker and come up with ideas to create a more manageable organization system.

Locker Organization

. . .

It's your job to keep track of all of your materials and set them up in a way where you can find everything. Going through these questions will support you in coming up with a good organization system for your locker.

What items need to be in your locker?

_____

_____

What are the most important items in your locker? Which ones do you use at least once a day?

_____

_____

What accessories would help you to better organize your locker?

_____

_____

Which way will you face your binders so you can see them best: stacked or facing outward?

_____

_____

How about your notebooks?

_____

_____

And folders?

_____

_____

What will you keep the rest of your supplies in (pencils, markers, pens, ruler, etc.)?

_____

_____

Taking Charge of Homework

Learning how to manage time spent on responsibilities, at work, and on schoolwork is a life skill that many people struggle to master. Daily homework is often the first opportunity students have to learn and practice this important skill. For students who have executive functioning difficulties with regard to planning and organization, planning the time (and order) in which they will complete their homework can be especially challenging, and they will benefit from more explicit instruction.

By developing an overall plan for completing their homework, students can maximize their effort and success, and they'll gain more control over the time that they spend working. This frees up larger blocks of time that they can spend as they wish, while ensuring that the time they do spend working is most productive. The plan creates a beginning and an end, so that students can see the light at the end of the tunnel.

We recommend that you engage parents in active discussions regarding the role you suggest they play in supporting their children throughout the homework process. In Cindy's parenting practice she finds that many parents are ill-equipped to support their children in developing good homework management practices. As a result, there is often tremendous stress and angst that develops between the parent and the child. Parents may look to over-help or push the expectations for quality work beyond the teachers expectations.

The following pages contain handouts and worksheets to help students plan ahead and take charge of homework. Some of the handouts will be best done by the student with their parents direct help, depending on the age of the student.

> "By failing to prepare, you are preparing to fail."
> – Benjamin Franklin

Plan for the Week

The first step in effectively making a homework plan is knowing when and how much time you have available to commit to your work. On the following page, use the "Plan for the Week" chart to write down any commitments that you know about. Be sure to include any doctor's appointments, lessons, or other outside obligations. Each week might be different, so you will want to fill out a new sheet each week, perhaps on Saturday or Sunday. It might also be helpful to show this chart to your parents to make sure you haven't forgotten to include any important commitments.

Once you have filled in all your responsibilities for the week, you are ready to plan when you will do each homework assignment and how much time you will spend on each task. It is better to know up front when you will do each assignment, so you don't run out of time or energy unexpectedly. Planning the order in which you'll complete each assignment is also important. For example, some people like to start off by tackling the harder or less interesting work first, so they feel that it is "behind" them. Others prefer to build momentum and cross things off their list by doing the easy, more engaging work first. Either approach is perfectly fine; it just depends on what works for you.

Once you have decided how long each task should take and what order you will do the work, you can use the "Pomodoro Planner" (p. 31) to break down your assignments into manageable intervals. Planning out your pomodoros should take no longer than five minutes, and it will help you decide when you will take your breaks. Remember, breaks can boost your ability to work effectively and efficiently, but make sure you keep them planned and limited so you can have your free time too.

Plan for the Week

• • •

Plan for the Week of _____

	Monday	Tuesday	Wednesday	Thursday	Friday	Saturday/ Sunday
3:00 – 3:30 pm						
3:30 – 4:00 pm						
4:00 – 4:30 pm						
4:30 – 5:00 pm						
5:00 – 5:30 pm						
5:30 – 6:00 pm						
6:00 – 6:30 pm						
6:30 – 7:00 pm						
7:00 – 7:30 pm						
7:30 – 8:00 pm						
8:00 – 8:30 pm						

Time Management

We each have many responsibilities in our lives, and the more efficient we are in getting done what it is that we need to do, the less stress we experience and the more free time that we have. Therefore, learning how to effectively manage our time is a valuable skill that we need to use our whole lives. One way to learn this skill is to practice managing time when it comes to doing homework and other responsibilities.

Like money, time is limited. **You can't use more than you have, and you can't get it back once you use it.** The better we become at budgeting both, the more flexibility we can have in making certain choices.

In order to learn about time management, please complete the following two activities in collaboration with your parent: "How Long Does It Really Take?" and "Where Does Your Time Go?" These two activities are intended to help you see how your time is actually "spent." Once you have completed these activities, you will be better prepared to approach managing homework and other responsibilities, and you will ultimately become a more effective time manager.

How Long Does It Really Take?

• • •

The purpose of this activity is to help you see how accurately you can predict or anticipate how long a given activity or assignment will take. When you estimate and time yourself for a particular task, make sure to include *all* of the components required to complete the activity. For example, don't forget steps such as gathering supplies, writing headers and questions, reading the material, doing things neatly, etc. In addition, make sure to use a timer or stopwatch to record the *exact* time it takes you to complete each activity.

After you complete each activity, please calculate the difference between how long you anticipated the activity would take and how long it actually took. See if you can determine whether you should be adjusting your time estimate, or perhaps the pace at which you do the activity. In addition, give some thought as to whether there are times of the day when it is easier for you to focus and be productive. Work within those times whenever possible! You will appreciate the free time it allows.

Task	Estimated Completion Time	Actual Completion Time	Time Difference	Notes
1.				
2.				
3.				
4.				

Task	Estimated Completion Time	Actual Completion Time	Time Difference	Notes
5.				
6.				
7.				
8.				
9				
10				
11				
12				

Where Does Your Time Go?

• • •

Sometimes, it feels like you'll have plenty of time to complete your responsibilities only to find that the day has ended without any time to spare. Do you ever wonder where all that time went? By tracking your known responsibilities, you will be better able to anticipate and plan the time that you have.

Hours per Week Needed for Basic Responsibilities	Hours
Number of hours per week you need to sleep to feel fully rested	
Number of hours per week spent eating meals	
Number of hours per week used for personal grooming (e.g., showering, brushing teeth, etc.)	
Number of hours per week used for "household" duties (e.g., laundry, cleaning, chores)	
Number of hours per week spent in class	
Number of hours per week spent at work	
Number of hours per week spent on physical fitness (e.g., practice with your sports team, working out at the gym)	
Number of hours per week spent commuting (between school, home, and work)	
Total Number of Hours Needed for Basic Responsibilities Each Week	

Hours per Week Needed for Schoolwork and Studying
(Reading, Exams, Papers, etc.)

	Hours
Course 1:	
Course 2:	
Course 3:	
Course 4:	
Course 5:	
Course 6:	
Total Number of Study Hours Needed Each Week	

Hours Remaining for Leisure

24 × 7 = 168 hours in the week	168
Subtract Number of Basic Responsibility Hours	
Subtract Number of Study Hours	
This is the number of hours available for leisure time	

To manage time, you must know how you spend it!

Taking Charge of Homework

...

There are several different ways to keep track of the schoolwork that you are responsible for doing. While some of the work may be listed on your school's website, you'll also be assigned work that needs to be tracked individually. Whether you decide to keep track of your assignments using a smartphone, tablet, computer, or agenda pad, it is helpful to have a list of all the work that you need to do in one, comprehensive place.

On the following page is an organizer called "Taking Charge of Homework," which contains all of the important components that you'll need in order to effectively plan out all of your assignments. The following instructions will help you get started in filling out the organizer:

1. For each of your class subjects, write down any assignments in the **center column**. You will notice that there are also separate lines for quizzes, tests, and projects. These lines are intended for you to write down what you need to study for a quiz or test, or any tasks that you need to complete to move forward with a class project.

2. In the **left-hand column**, record what you need to bring home from school for each subject. When you go to your locker at the end of the day, be sure to check off that you have everything you need.

3. There are also times when you may need support from a teacher, parent, or friend to complete a specific task. Before you begin your work, look over each assignment briefly and see if you will need help. If so, make arrangements with that person and write it down in the space provided.

4. Finally, in the **right-hand column**, estimate how long you anticipate that each task will take. This is crucial as you prepare to plan out how you will manage your homework for that day. If you are unsure how long the assignment should take, ask your teacher or a friend.

5. When filling out the chart, you may find that by using some consistent abbreviations, you can reduce the time needed to record your work. For example, "R" means "Read," "Pg" means "Page," and "W" means "Write."

Taking Charge of Homework

...

CLASS SUBJECTS

WORK TO BE DONE...

HOW LONG WILL IT TAKE?

Math

Materials needed:

Do you have materials needed?

Will you need help?

With whom and how long?

Homework:

Quiz:

Test:

Project:

Time:

Homework:

Quiz:

Test:

Project:

English

Materials needed:

Do you have materials needed?

Will you need help?

With whom and how long?

Homework

Quiz:

Test:

Project:

Time:

Homework:

Quiz:

Test:

Project:

ESTIMATE HOW LONG IT WILL TAKE?

Time:
- Homework:
- Quiz:
- Test:
- Project:

Time:
- Homework:
- Quiz:
- Test:
- Project:

Time:
- Homework:
- Quiz:
- Test:
- Project:

WORK TO BE DONE …

Homework:
- Quiz:
- Test:
- Project:

Homework:
- Quiz:
- Test:
- Project:

Homework:
- Quiz:
- Test:
- Project:

CLASS SUBJECTS

Science
- Materials needed:
- Do you have materials needed?
- Will you need help?
- With whom and how long?

Social Studies
- Materials needed:
- Do you have materials needed?
- Will you need help?
- With whom and how long?

Language
- Materials needed:
- Do you have materials needed?
- Will you need help?
- With whom and how long?

Shorthand: R – Read • W – Write • Pg – Page • Bk – Book • Br – Binder • C – Calculator

When Assignments Are Not Completed

There will be times when students do not turn in their homework as expected or required. For students who have ADHD or executive function challenges, the reason the work is not completed may not always be apparent, especially when parents intervene from time to time without your knowledge. Students may have had the homework assignment written down but may have forgotten the materials needed to do the assignment. Remember, organization may be part of their challenges. They may also have lost focus during a crucial point in the lesson, or may not have been able to keep up with the information being presented due to a slower processing speed or weak working memory, as we will talk about shortly. Or they may have been triggered emotionally, either by frustration with the assignment, lack of confidence, or any number of factors that may have happened once leaving school. It is valuable for students to learn to advocate for themselves and to feel safe enough to do so. Otherwise, they sometimes resort to other methods of compensating, such as cheating, lying, or just shutting down. If you notice a pattern of missed or incomplete homework, or work that is not consistent with the level of understanding the student seems to demonstrate in the classroom, it may signal that some investigation is necessary so you can see if the student needs accommodations, modifications, or some other support.

Of course, there are times when students do not complete the required work because of poor decision-making or lack of appropriate effort. **The two worksheets that follow may be useful at these times.**

If you notice that there is significant friction between the parents and the child regarding schoolwork, this tension can greatly impact the social and emotional growth of the child, as well as their performance in school and other activities. Our main message to parents: **Never let your relationship suffer at the altar of schoolwork!** When parents and students are in constant battle, everyone loses. We suggest that parents work with teachers and perhaps get assistance from counselors and possibly tutors to help address the causes of the tension and brainstorm solutions to address the core issues.

Student Choice Form

. . .

Today's Date: _____

I, _____ , have chosen not to

complete the _____ assignment that was due on _____.

I understand that by making this choice, I may be less prepared to understand and learn future lessons that this assignment builds upon.

I understand that by not doing this assignment, I am choosing to receive a lower grade at the end of the marking period.

I understand that I am still responsible for mastering the information that I had the opportunity to learn during homework.

I understand that if I feel that I cannot manage this work, then I may ask for help from my teacher and other outside supports. I am responsible for asking for help, and I am allowed to ask for it if I need to. It is my right and my obligation.

Student Signature: _____

Parent Signature: _____

Oops! I Did Not Complete My Homework for Today

• • •

Check all that apply:

____ I forgot to do my assignment.

____ I chose not to do my assignment.

____ I was not feeling well enough to do the assignment.

____ I was absent and didn't receive the materials I needed to do the assignment.

____ I forgot to bring the correct materials home. (I forgot: _____.)

____ I did not know how to do the assignment. (Specify where you got stuck: _____

_____.)

____ Other reason. (Explain in detail: _____.)

My plan for next time is:

_____

_____

Student Signature: _____

Parent Signature: _____

Date: _____

#4: REGULATING ALERTNESS, SUSTAINING EFFORT, AND PROCESSING SPEED

The ability to stay alert and engaged is a skill that many people take for granted. However, it is something that people with ADHD can really struggle with whenever they must engage in a task that is not intrinsically interesting or that does not provide them with enough active stimulation. This problem in regulating alertness plays a dual role in individuals with ADHD (Brown, 2008): On the one hand, individuals with ADHD frequently report experiencing drowsiness when they must complete uninteresting or under-stimulating tasks, *even when they have actually gotten enough rest*. On the other hand, these impairments in regulating alertness also make it difficult for them to fall asleep at night, which causes true issues with exhaustion that interfere with their ability to complete tasks.

In addition to problems in regulating alertness, individuals with ADHD often struggle to sustain effort on tasks. It is heightened interest that generates the release of dopamine in the brain and sustains the level for as long as the intensified interest persists. People with ADHD often struggle when they find the task uninteresting.

Lastly, individuals with ADHD exhibit impairments in processing speed, which involves how quickly and efficiently people can complete a task with reasonable accuracy. Processing speed can be broken down into three components, which involve how quickly we can (1) take in information, (2) process that information, and (3) respond to that information. People can also vary how they process verbal and visual information, and how they respond when motor coordination is involved. For everyone, processing speed is sensitive to anxiety, stress, and pressure. However, for those with ADHD, these impairments are more pervasive, and they can create some of the most significant challenges in learning and performing. When it takes longer to process information, it understandably takes longer to solve problems, respond to situations, and function as desired or expected.

Impairments in processing speed can affect a student's ability to read, complete math problems, listen and take notes, make decisions, and participate in group discussions. Students who have difficulty with processing speed often struggle to complete their work on time not because they don't understand the material, but because it takes them longer to read through the directions and answer the questions. Often, they also stop paying attention in class because they can't keep pace with the lesson. In fact, slow processing speed can impact all of the other branches of executive functioning.

Processing Speed and Intelligence

One important point to consider is that there is **no relationship between processing speed and intelligence**. You can have a very high IQ and still have impaired processing speed. We believe this is a vital point for all students and parents to understand: Speed does not equal intelligence. However, even as early as preschool, children often assume that it does. When young children are in class and a teacher asks them a question, how do children classify which students are "smart"? They assume that the smart students are the ones who raise their hands quickly, get called on, and have the correct answer.

To illustrate the problem with this assumption regarding intelligence, we want you to imagine for a moment that you are in kindergarten and the teacher points to the following object and asks, "What is the black shape called?"

Now, some students will immediately raise their hands and respond with, "That's a circle." In turn, the teacher will state, "That's right, and who knows what shape is inside the circle?" However, a student with a slower processing speed may still be processing the first question ("What is the black shape called?") and, in turn, may not have raised his or her hand in time. At the same time, another student who is struggling just to stay focused on the task at hand may be thinking, "That's cool, there is a triangle on the inside of a circle, and inside that there is a letter. I know that letter; it's the letter 'A.'" This student, while certainly very intelligent, may also not have raised his or her hand quickly enough to be called on since the student was busy having an internal dialogue. That student may also assume that others are experiencing the same internal dialogue but were still able to answer the teacher's question when asked. This belief may lead this student to incorrectly conclude that he or she is not as smart as the others who answered correctly in a more timely manner.

Supporting Students with Slower Processing Speed

Slower processing speed is not like a learning disability that can be remediated. Rather, **the best approach is to provide supports and accommodations.** The following are some supports and ideas for the classroom to help students with some of these challenges. As always, keep in mind that every student is unique, and that different strategies will work for different students, regardless of whether they have challenges in processing speed.

1. **Allow students extended time on assignments, tests, and, quizzes.** For many students, 1.5 time on a test will make a big difference in their ability to be successful. Taking away time restrictions will give students with slower processing speed a chance to have their knowledge tested rather than their processing speed.

2. **Minimize the amount of "clerical tasks" that students need to complete.** For example, do not require students to copy notes from one space to another, or ask to them copy down a list of spelling words that could otherwise be printed.

3. **Reduce the number of tasks required for students to demonstrate competence.** For example, reduce the required number of questions that students must answer on worksheets, or reduce the number of examples that students need to give in order to show their understanding of a topic.

4. **Increase the level of scaffolding on assignments.** For example, help students get started by breaking a task down into more concrete pieces. When directing a student to answer a written response question, you may add instructions for students to include specific vocabulary words in their response.

5. **Consider eliminating timed tests, such as "Mad Math Minutes."** Group tests (particularly those that are conducted using timed drills) can be very frustrating and create anxiety for students who have executive function challenges. Consider finding ways to have students work on fact fluency while allowing varying expectations for different students, such as personalized goals.

6. **Limit the amount of time that students spend on homework.** For example, require that students work on a given assignment for a maximum of 20 minutes. Let them know that they will be graded on what they complete, not on how much they complete.

7. **Allow the whole class a few seconds to consider their answer before allowing them to raise their hands.** For example, you may say, "In a few moments I will ask you to raise your hand if you know who

the first president was." This allows everyone to focus on formulating their answer rather than feeling pressure as some start to raise their hands.

8. **Provide students with an outline of the lesson or notes.** This can be valuable for all students, but especially for students who struggle to write quickly enough or have trouble focusing on listening while they are writing.

#5: UTILIZING WORKING MEMORY AND ACCESSING RECALL

Imagine the following scenario. You tell your class, "Okay, everyone, take out your notebooks, calculators, and protractors, and turn to page 42 in your math textbook. Start working on problem number 7." As you look around, you observe that some of the students are busy working. However, one or two students are somewhat in a daze, maybe looking around to figure out what everyone is doing, or just sitting with their notebooks and calculators out. To the untrained eye, these students may appear lazy, unmotivated, or even defiant. While many of those things may be true, it may also be true that these students have weaker working memory and were not able to hold on to the information needed to begin their work.

Working memory is the "mental workspace" where we *temporarily* store, retain, and manipulate information. It requires the ability to use the brain's "search engine" to hold on to and manipulate new information, while the brain figures out if it can connect this information to more long-term storage. Whether or not you realize it, working memory is a skill that you use in your everyday life. For example, when someone gives you the directions to their house, your working memory allows you to store that information as you get to their address. Similarly, you use your working memory when you hear a new phone number and must hold it in your mind as you dial it into the phone. You even use your working memory when you engage in conversations with others to follow along with what they have said.

However, people with ADHD often have impairments in working memory that interfere with their ability to effectively engage in such tasks. Students with weak working memory may struggle to retain information they hear, see, or read. This can lead to struggles in all areas of learning, such as remembering instructions, characters, or facts in a story, or information needed for word problems in math. It can also impact their ability to learn to read, recognize, and reproduce patterns that are the building blocks for learning mathematical formulas. For example, when a student is reading a story, he may be able to hold on to information and facts that he is interested in since he is paying close attention. However, if he is not as interested, he may not focus as intently and integrate the information into his working memory. Then when it is time to answer questions about the text he can talk about the areas that were interesting to him, however, miss some of the big ideas that he was not paying attention to as closely.

Deficits in working memory can certainly create tremendous challenges for students. However, just like many other skills, working memory is a skill that can be strengthened with practice. **The following are some simple games that you can play with your students to support them in building their working memory.** These games find engaging and motivating ways to get students to practice using their memory by holding on to facts and making connections in their environment.

Three Cups

• • •

All you will need for this game is three cups (bowls can work too) and one small object that fits underneath. Place the object underneath one of the cups, making sure to show the student which cup you have placed it under. Then, move the cups around into different positions. After scrambling the cups around a bit, ask the student to identify which cup the object is under.

Why does it help? Children have to hold on to the placement of the object in their head and use their working memory to follow your movements.

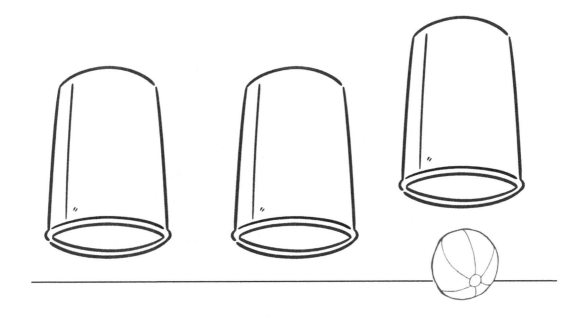

What's Different on Me?

• • •

This very simple and quick game is excellent to play with younger children. Give students a chance to examine how you look. Then, have them close their eyes as you change one thing about your appearance (e.g., untie your shoe, remove an accessory, etc.). After students open their eyes, ask them to identify what you changed.

Why does it help? Children must hold on to what they saw before they closed their eyes and use their working memory to examine what changed.

Story Chain

• • •

Verbally make up a story with your students where everyone takes a turn adding on a short phrase to the story. Begin with a "story starter" phrase, and then ask students to repeat the story starter and continuing adding on to it. The story goes on until someone can't remember what has come before. The following are some examples of how a story chain could unfold.

> Yesterday I went to the park and…
> > It started to rain!
> > It was wet
> > and cold.
> > I decided to dance!

> I think it will snow tomorrow so…
> > I hope we
> > have a snow day!
> > If we do,
> > I'll play outside
> > and go sledding
> > and make snow angels.

Why does it help? Students will have fun coming up with a creative story while using their working memory to remember what happened before in the story and use this information to add on more.

Matching Memory-Games

· · ·

Memory-matching games are very common games where students must remember something that they have seen and find the matching pair. First, shuffle the cards and lay them face up on a surface. After the student has had some time to look at the cards, turn over all the cards face down. Then, have the student choose two cards from the set that he or she thinks are a matching pair. Memory-matching games come in many varieties that match the needs or interests of your students. You can also use playing cards or patterns like those below.

Why does it help? Students have to hold the card image in their mind and use their working memory to recall this information to find the matching pair.

#6: SELF-MONITORING

Self-monitoring involves being able to use self-talk to monitor and regulate one's behavior, as well as to direct future actions. Using self-talk is a vital component involved in planning and problem solving. However, students with ADHD have difficulty with self-monitoring. They have trouble using forethought to restrain their actions, which leads them to act impulsively.

Individuals who have difficulty self-monitoring also don't seem to notice external social cues that inform how they should act. For example, they may struggle to identify when and how to interrupt, tell a joke, or advocate for themselves. They may also have a difficult time recognizing how others perceive them, or they might be overly self-conscious about how others view them. As a result, they may appear socially ineffective or even inappropriate.

You can help students develop a more active internal dialogue by having them witness how you use self-talk. For example, as teachers, you can tell them the process you went through in deciding how you would teach a particular lesson. You might even share examples of times when you thought about your plan, decided it may not work, and adjusted to make a new plan. Similarly, next time you want your students to prepare for math, rather than saying, "Okay, everyone, take out your pencils, rulers, and note paper," you may just say, "It's time for math, what should you do?" Then, give the students a moment to think. Of course, if the task involves multiple steps or objects, remember to support those with working-memory challenges by using visual aids or repetition.

The following section contains activities that are intended to help students recognize their own self-talk and increase their awareness of how to use self-talk to motivate themselves and stay focused.

Change Your Words

Words are powerful. They have a significant impact on how we feel and what we accomplish. In the exact same situation, we can frame our language positively, or we can frame it negatively. The underlying meaning might actually be the same, but the language we choose to use has a genuine impact on what happens next. Stating that you are not good at something sets the tone that you have given up on being successful at it. However, if you change your words to say that you are still working at being good at it, then it may still be true *in this moment* that you are not good at it, but now you have implied that you are capable of getting better.

Getting in the practice of using positive language allows us to get through challenging situations more easily and simply stay in a better mood. However, if we are used to using negative language, then we can be shut down easily by a challenge and quickly resort to feeling defeated.

Anxiousness, fear, and doubt are emotions just like calmness, courage, and confidence. The language we use when we talk to ourselves is powerful. At times, negative language comes more naturally, and positive talk has to be practiced a bit more. **The following two worksheet and exercise give students a chance to come up with words or phrases that they can insert when they might be tempted to use negative language.** Having these phrases handy—and getting in the habit of using them more often—will allow positive self-talk to start coming more naturally and help students reframe their thinking in a positive, more productive way.

Change Your Words

• • •

The language you use really matters. The words you say have a real impact on the way you feel and the things you accomplish. The negative thoughts we have are the ones that can shut us down and decide the outcome. Changing your language to "positive thoughts" leaves optimistic openings and creates space for you to improve. You may want to add a few negative thoughts of your own in addition to the ones provided. Then, use the right-hand column to reframe each negative thought into a positive thought.

Negative Thoughts	Positive Thoughts
I'm not good at this.	Example: I will need to practice this a few times.
This is too hard.	
I hate writing.	
I give up.	
I failed.	
This is dumb.	
I don't care.	
I've already tried this.	
I'll never be good at…	

Shield Yourself
with Positive Self-Talk

• • •

Negative self-talk can happen in those moments when we are feeling stressed or anxious. Maybe we are in a new situation or working on a task that we often have a tough time with. This negative language only serves to make the situation more challenging and can make our mind shut down altogether. We can battle through this negative self-talk by practicing and being prepared with positive phrases to insert instead.

Instructions:

Fill in the sunglasses below with positive thoughts that shield you from any negative thoughts that try to enter your mind.

#7: EMOTION REGULATION

Emotion regulation is the ability to understand and accept your emotional experience, to manage your emotions, and to respond with behavior that is appropriate *in that moment.* In the school environment, students must engage in emotion regulation on a daily basis. For example, they need to manage how they react to disappointing grades, struggles with their peers, and expectations that they may find frustrating, boring, or too challenging.

However, students with ADHD struggle to regulate their emotions, particularly in situations involving stress or frustration. These students who may appear highly sensitive and overreactive. They may appear emotionally impulsive, as they may go from being calm to melting down or becoming enraged in a matter of seconds. In particular, individuals with ADHD have a hard time with the following:

- Inhibiting their emotional reactions or responses
- Modulating their level of anger and expression of raw emotion
- Being patient
- Tolerating frustration
- Being flexible/adaptable
- Regulating their attention
- Refocusing their attention away from frustrating situations
- Calming themselves down or self-soothing

However, keep in mind that students with ADHD have nothing "wrong" with their emotions. ADHD is not a mood disorder, but rather a disorder that is associated with difficulties in managing the expression of emotions. This makes it more challenging to teach, parent, and in many cases, establish balanced, healthy relationships with individuals with ADHD.

The following section contains several activities that can help students gain a better understanding of their emotions, as well as exercises to help them build empathy and take others' perspective. In addition to these tools, the most valuable way to support students who struggle with emotion regulation is through a collaborative problem-solving process, which is outlined in Chapter 4.

Mind-Body Connection

When we are feeling a bit out of control, it helps to have a better understanding of our emotions. One way for your students to understand their own feelings is to teach them how different feelings in their body are connected to different emotions. For example, some people experience anger as a feeling of heat all over their body, but they experience anxiety as a feeling of butterflies in their stomach.

Sometimes, when students experience different feelings in their body but aren't sure what they mean, they might have a harder time managing their emotional responses. By helping them gain an understanding of what various feelings mean, we can better equip students to handle different emotions.

Identifying Your Feelings Worksheet

On the following worksheet, ask students to identify how different feelings manifest in their body. Start by having your students pick a color to connect with each emotion. Then, discuss each emotion in terms of how it might make your body feel. Have students use the color they chose for that emotion to color that area on their body. You also might want to allow students to change the darkness of their coloring to match how intense that feeling is when they have this emotion.

Identifying Your Feelings

• • •

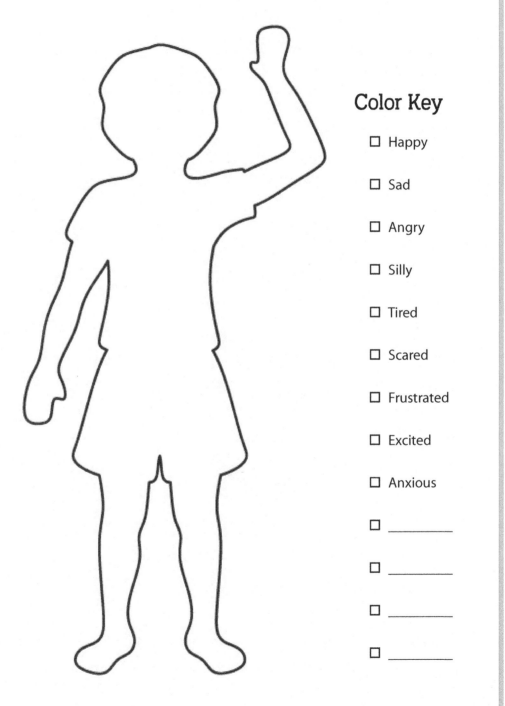

Color Key

☐ Happy

☐ Sad

☐ Angry

☐ Silly

☐ Tired

☐ Scared

☐ Frustrated

☐ Excited

☐ Anxious

☐ _____

☐ _____

☐ _____

☐ _____

How Do Our Bodies Respond to Emotions?

• • •

The following activity is another tool that students can use to identify the ways that their body looks and feels when they experience different emotions. First, ask students to draw what their face looks like when they feel a certain way. Then, have students identify what different parts of their body feel like when they experience this emotion. Finally, ask students to identify one thing that they should do when they are feeling this way.

Below is an example of this activity completed for the emotion of happiness, followed by a blank worksheet that you can give students.

Emotion: Happy

My eyes feel: Relaxed

My face feels: Comfortable

My hands feel: Loose

My feet feel: Relaxed

My stomach feels: Good

When I feel this way, I will: Keep doing what I am doing. It feels good to be happy!

How Do Our Bodies Respond to Emotions?

• • •

Instructions:

Using an emotion that you decide on or are given by your teacher, draw what your face might look like when you are feeling that way. Then, come up with a description of how different parts of your body feel when you are having this emotion.

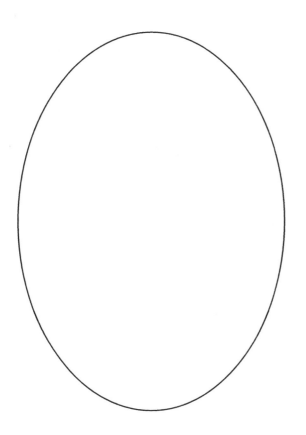

Emotion: _____

My Eyes Feel: _____

My Face Feels: _____

My Hands Feel: _____

My Feet Feel: _____

My Stomach Feels: _____

When I feel this way, I will: _____

_____

Calming Techniques

When students with ADHD feel angry, frustrated, or even silly, they might have a hard time coming backing from these moments, which can create further challenges. **The following list of techniques is a tool that you can use with students when they need strategies to calm their bodies and emotions. We created this to provide you with a variety of options that your students can experiment with when they need extra help calming down.** Every child is different, and many children will need a few different strategies from which to choose. Feel free to try out a few different strategies and allow your students to determine what works best for them.

Calming Techniques

• • •

Star Breathing

Balloon Breathing

Journal/Write

Take a Walk

Reading a Book

Go to a Calming Corner

Star breathing is a simple technique that gives students something to focus on while they work to calm their breathing. Using the star image on the next page, have your students trace the star as they breathe in going up to a point, and out, going down from a point.

Balloon breathing, also known as belly breathing, is another simple breathing technique to help students slow down their breathing. Have students place their hand on their belly as they breathe in and out. They should feel their belly rise (like an inflating balloon) when they breathe in, and they should feel it go down (like letting air out of a balloon) when they breathe out.

For some students, **journaling or writing** can serve as an excellent strategy for calming down. Whether it allows them to "mind dump" and let go of negative thoughts, or allows them to think through a stressful situation, journaling or writing can be a useful and simple tool to use.

Going for a walk can be an easy and simple way to regulate our emotions. Help students effectively use this strategy by setting clear boundaries for where walks occur (e.g., to the nurse's office and back). You might want to create a walking pass that students can take when they need to calm down with a walk.

Some students benefit from having a nice quiet space with a book they can **read** in order to help reset them. This is a great tool that students can use independently when they need to regain control of their emotions.

Many students just need **a safe and quiet space** away from a stressful or hectic situation. Designate an area in your room as a "calming corner" where students can go if they need to calm down. A few sensory tools, like stress balls or pillows, can help create a space where students can reset.

Star Breathing

• • •

Instructions:

Starting at the top point of the star, trace the outside of the star while breathing in down to a point, and breathing out towards the next point. Continue to breathe in and out around the star until you feel your body breathing slowly and in control.

FLEXIBLE THINKING

Part of having strong emotion regulation skills involves being flexible when changes occur or when we don't get our way. For a student who struggles with emotional regulation, being flexible can be very challenging. We often see this with our students who have ADHD, as they become increasingly frustrated when their flexibility is challenged. For example, there might be a last-minute change in schedule, or it's time for an activity to end before students are finished with the assignment. These moments can lead to emotional outbursts or defiant behaviors for students with poor emotion regulation skills. By teaching students about flexible thinking, we can help them better manage these frustrating situations.

The following three exercises are intended to help your students develop flexible thinking. The first exercise teaches students about the different aspects of being flexible versus rigid, including the benefits of flexibility and the downsides of rigidity. Once students have developed a stronger understanding of some of the different qualities of flexibility and rigidity, the second activity gives them a chance to continue exploring this idea while seeing how it impacts their body. Finally, the third exercise helps students practice being flexible by asking them to come up with a variety of ways that they can complete certain tasks. Although it will be reasonably easy for students to come up with the first idea, the real challenge of this activity is coming up with two additional ways to complete each task.

How Much Can It Stretch?

. . .

This activity is intended to teach students the importance of flexible thinking. Part of regulating emotions means being willing to stretch our thinking and handle situations that don't go our way. By teaching students about the importance of being flexible, and the benefits they gain from flexibility, we can help students build on this critical skill.

Materials:

- Flexible items (rubber bands, playdough, pipe cleaners, etc.)
- Rigid items (popsicle sticks, toothpicks, uncooked spaghetti, etc.)

Instructions:

1. Allow the students to explore the materials, and work with them to determine which are flexible and which are rigid. Discuss the qualities of rigid and flexible items.

2. Have the students chose a flexible item and a rigid item, and ask them to try and make two arches (one flexible arch and one rigid arch). Discuss which arch was easier to make and why this is the case.

3. Have a discussion around which items would be easier to break and which would be able to withstand more stretching. Allow a few students to demonstrate trying to break some of the flexible items and the rigid items.

4. Conclude by discussing what the students noticed about the benefits of being flexible compared to the downsides of being rigid. Ask the students how they can benefit from being flexible in the classroom. What might be some consequences of being rigid in school?

Flexible or Rigid: Which Is Better?

• • •

Instructions:

Follow the instructions above each box to experience the difference between doing something rigidly and doing something flexibly. As you go through this activity, think about some of the benefits and challenges of being rigid compared to being flexible. Then, answer questions about whether it's better to be flexible or rigid.

Keep your arm straight (rigid) and a draw a picture of a beach scene:

Now, try drawing the same picture but allow your arm to be looser (flexible) as you draw:

Which drawing was easier to do? Why?

_____

_____

Now, thinking outside of these drawings, would you rather be flexible or rigid?

_____

_____

Three Different Ways

...

Instructions:

Although it can sometimes seem that there is only one "right" way to do something, the reality is that there are often multiple ways to effectively complete a task. Some people have one way of doing things that works well for them, and others have a different way. What works well for one person may not work for someone else.

Think of three *different* ways that you can complete each of the tasks listed below. You can either write out your answers with words or draw them with pictures.

What are three ways to...

Pack a Backpack

1.   2.   3.

Organize Your Desk

1.   2.   3.

Study for a Test

1.   2.   3.

Manage Your Homework

1.   2.   3.

Write a First Draft

1.   2.   3.

Getting Unstuck

There will come a time when students are unsure of how to proceed with a homework assignment. It could be that they are confused about what is being asked, where to find certain resources, etc. For students with emotion regulation difficulties, this "stuck" feeling can sometimes lead to them feeling shut down, even if the solution to the problem is fairly easy to find.

Having a resource for these students to go to during these "stuck" moments can minimize their frustration and keep them moving forward so they can get their homework done. **The following worksheet is intended to help students when they need assistance with a homework assignment and are not in school.** It can be used when they have a question about what they should be doing, how they are expected to complete an assignment, where they can find certain materials, or other related questions.

When I Get Stuck

• • •

Instructions:

At times, we come to a point when we might get stuck on work at home. You might be unsure of where to find a resource, or forget what the teacher has asked for on an assignment. Come up with ideas and strategies for what you can do during these times when you get stuck.

Things I can do when I get stuck: _____

_____

_____

Strategies I have:

1. _____
2. _____
3. _____
4. _____
5. _____

Online resources:

1. _____
2. _____
3. _____
4. _____
5. _____

Possible resources for homework help: class friends, teachers, tutors

Name	Phone number	Email address

What to Do if You Suspect a Student has ADHD or Executive Function Deficits

Imagine that you have a student in your class who struggles to stay on task in the classroom. She constantly interrupts class lectures and blurts out answers without raising her hand. Or perhaps she remains quiet and seems to behave fine; however, does not turn in work and isn't performing up to expectations. If you are a teacher, having a student in your classroom who exhibits these behaviors is a common reality. So, what do you do?

While every school has a different policy, one universal practice is that teachers *should not* suggest to the child's parent that the student may have ADHD or any other diagnosable condition. However, the teacher can, in meeting with a parent, provide helpful information that reinforces the teacher's concerns and that supports an assessment of the student's challenges beyond the classroom. Teachers may want to gather some specific examples that reflect their concerns. But be careful. In doing so, it's easy to have the conversation unintentionally take off in the wrong direction, as in the following examples:

Teacher: I notice that Sara often has a difficult time paying attention.

Parent: Well, I assume you help her with that?

Teacher: I notice that Jonny is struggling to get himself organized.

Parent: I know, I tell him all the time that he is such a slob.

Teacher: Sam often calls out in class and sometimes is chatty with other students while they are doing their work.

Parent: I am so disappointed in him. I am going to have to talk with him about this tonight.

The best way to give parents information about your concerns is to focus on developmental expectations and class-wide norms, and to then share how the student differs from those norms. For example:

- By second or third grade, you should expect students to follow safety rules, raise their hand before speaking, and keep their hands to themselves.
- By sixth or seventh grade, you should expect students to use a system for organizing their schoolwork and to follow a schedule that includes changing classrooms and teachers.
- By high school, students should be able to create and follow timelines for long-term projects, and to also adjust their level of effort and the quality of their work in response to feedback from teachers and others.

It is valuable to seek the input and observations of other teachers and staff, who can help you see whether different variables may be impacting the student's performance. For example, consider whether any of the following variables have an impact on the:

- Time of day
- Student's interest in the subject matter
- Student's confidence level
- Student's ability level
- Whether the student's friends are in the class (and, if so, whether that is helpful or serves as a deterrent)
- Teacher's structure level

Be cautious in assuming that a student's behavior may be due to immaturity, gender, perceived motivation, or parenting techniques (teachers don't ever really know what goes on at home and the challenges parents genuinely face). Having said that, though, don't ignore the voice in your gut. As a trained, experienced professional, you see many students at the same time, so your perspective of individual differences provides important information.

Just be careful not to use words that imply that you are diagnosing the student. In addition, remember to seek the input, concerns, and observations of the parent because—as we said early on—challenges can show up differently in different settings.

While there are formal measures of executive function, the best way to assess a student's executive functioning abilities is to conduct individual, structured interviews with the parent, student, and other teachers. Here are some helpful questions:

- How does the student handle goal setting, making decisions, and planning?
- How is the student at regulating his or her attention, getting started on work, and staying with the task until it's complete?
- How well does the student handle their materials?
- How efficiently does the student manage their time?
- How effectively does the student manage multiple steps and details?
- How well does the student manage their impulses and emotional reactions?
- How flexible and adaptable is the student when a change or the unexpected occurs?

In asking these questions, you are not looking for merely "good vs. bad" answers. Rather, you are looking for detailed descriptions and examples. **Remember, the purpose of the interview is to gather helpful information, not to make a diagnosis.** Keep in mind that the benefit of such a discussion is to give you a starting place to see what the student needs to learn to function more effectively. It also will help you decide the best ways to intervene, including whether you need to:

- Change the environment
- Provide targeted accommodations
- Provide specific modifications
- Provide more or different supports

EDUCATING PARENTS

Parents who are more informed about what impacts learning, motivation, and behavior are going to be your best partners in supporting the education of your students. They have a vital purpose that they play in helping all students learn, manage, and perform in school. Teaching students and parents about executive functioning is beneficial. As mentioned earlier in this chapter, we often refer to the executive functions as the CEO of the brain. Therefore, one important part of teaching students about executive functioning involves helping them recognize when their "managers" may need a bit more training or support. This approach can take away some of the shame and deficit, and instead focus on skill building.

Another important thing to consider is *who* the CEO of the brain is at various stages of development. For example, in elementary school the parents and educators often are the CEO of the students' brains. These are the individuals helping students manage different transitions, materials, expectations, etc. However, as students move to middle school, they become more independent and often follow the norms set by their peer group. In this respect, it's as if students' peers become the CEO of the brain at this stage of development. Finally, once students enter high school, many appear ready to take on the role of CEO. However, many students *feel* readier than they actually are for the many expectations and responsibilities that they need to manage. This discrepancy creates some of the push-pull experienced by parents of students who struggle with executive functioning challenges. Their children may claim, "I've got this," even though the evidence does not entirely support that statement.

Working with Parents

Working with parents is often more complex than it may initially seem. After all, is it their first child? Only child? Are the parents comparing this child to their other child, who may be unusually easy or unusually challenging? There may also be significant stressors at home, such as financial struggles, health concerns, and marital strife. Parents may disagree on how best to approach their child's struggles—one wants to be stricter, and one wants to be more lenient. There may also be cultural differences that make it taboo to seek out services and receive support. And don't forget: ADHD is highly heritable, so the child's parent(s) may be undiagnosed with the condition or lack the skills needed themselves.

It's also not just about the parent—imagine the student's day! Most students with ADHD are more sensitive to their environment, expectations, and experiences. It often takes students with ADHD much more effort to achieve the same amount of work than it does their peers. They must constantly put forth effort to regulate their emotions, motivation, and attention—which can really drain their ability to handle frustration, expectations, and experiences. By the time they get home from school, they are out of emotional fuel, and they (and their parents) may be unequipped to manage what comes next—homework!

ENABLING VS. SUPPORTING

Parents and educators often struggle when it comes to deciding whether or not to provide a student with an accommodation or modification. In giving a student a "leg up" or a "crutch" are we making them more dependent? Are we preventing them from trying their best? Are we giving them a message that they aren't capable of reaching their peer's standards? These are important distinctions and not always easy to determine.

One way to address this issue is to look at how we define enabling versus supporting. When we ask parents and educators to define enabling I get answers such as these:

- When we don't expect the child to do what they could do, or should do, on their own.
- When we make excuses for a child, who has acted poorly, or not done as they are expected to do.
- When we "over help" or "fix" the work the child has done.
- When we don't allow the natural consequences of their behavior to occur.

If a child forgets to bring in their violin for the 3rd time this month and the parent brings it to school in time for orchestra, is this parent enabling the child? It may appear that way at first, but let's consider another possibility.

Perhaps, the student knows that she must finish her homework before practicing the violin. And, of course, it takes a long time to complete homework (or anything) for this child. So, trying to be good, she goes downstairs and practices until her dad says "Come up, Mary, it's time to shower and get ready for bed." So, Mary leaves her violin, planning to pack up after the shower. And… next morning Dad goes downstairs after Mary leaves for school and *there is the violin.* "What should I do?" he thinks. "I don't want her to get in trouble. And I know she isn't great about being organized—in fact, it's not my strong suit either sometimes. And gee, she made the bus today! And her shoes matched! Ok, her room is a mess, and she did fight with her sister. But we are working on those things. I guess I have to add getting organized for school to the list. Oh, that list is long—but the other things on there are more important right now. I think I'll just bring in the violin again and make a plan to help her—when we have time to focus on that issue.

Our definition of *enabling*: *Enabling is doing something for someone else without a PLAN to help them do it for themselves.*

Given that, perhaps before we judge from the outside that someone is "enabling," we may need to step back and recognize that we don't know what we don't know.

What do we suggest teachers do if they notice a pattern of behavior where the parents are being more involved than might seem expected or helpful? Say to the parent, "I see you are bringing in the violin again today. Is there anything I can do to help?" Sometimes, collaborating with the parent, and perhaps the student, can help the student develop a new, helpful structure or routine.

It is imperative for everyone working with children to understand what the executive functioning skills are and how the development of these skills impacts all aspects of a student's life. It is valuable to share information about executive function with parents and the concept that we are each the "CEO" of our brain's executive function system. Providing parents with a basic understanding of this will help them become familiar with the concepts you are teaching their children.

Our goal with the remaining chapters is to help you build students' awareness of the executive functions and to teach them the skills needed to become more effective "managers" of their brain.

If you sense that a student's parents need more than just these tools, it's possible that their child might benefit from a coach who specializes in providing ADHD and executive function coaching. Similarly, if you feel that a student has completely shut down and that parents are at a loss regarding how to reach or support their child, that parent might benefit from their own parent coaching (see www.PTScoaching.com for resources).

3. Communication:
Helping Students Connect Through Words

COMMUNICATION CHALLENGES IN ADHD

Many students (and adults ☺), especially those with ADHD and executive functioning challenges, struggle when it comes to expressing themselves, listening to others, taking others' perspectives, and managing the flow of a conversation. Some struggle with impulsivity that makes it especially challenging for them to wait their turn speaking. Others have low frustration tolerance—they need answers and want their needs met NOW. Still others deal with high levels of anxiety or inflexibility that dramatically impact what and how they communicate. Some may even appear as if they don't care about other people's perspectives since they are so focused on their own. Lastly, those who process things more slowly and have a weaker working memory may have difficulties navigating the pace and content of conversations.

To overcome these challenges, we have found that it can make a tremendous positive impact when we actively teach students *how* to have a beneficial conversation. By explicitly teaching these skills, students feel more confident that they can get their points across and are more able to confirm and demonstrate their understanding of what the speaker is communicating.

In the following section, we will outline three important factors involved in having a productive conversation: active listening, perspective taking, and appropriate ways to interrupt. Formally teaching students these skills will help them work more appropriately during small group projects, on the playground, or anytime that involves unstructured discussion.

MODELING AND TEACHING COMMUNICATION

The Role of the Listener

While most productive conversations have a random and natural flow, if you look closely, one person is generally listening as the other person is speaking. The person listening may interject, communicate nonverbally, agree, or disagree—but, generally, that person is focused on the story told by the speaker until it is appropriate to shift and become the speaker themselves. When we want to help students learn to be effective listeners during a conversation, it is helpful to dissect the different parts involved in being a listener: mirroring, validating, and empathizing.

Mirror what you hear. As you listen to the speaker, try to focus on understanding what they are saying and see if you can repeat back what you heard. You do not need to use the same words. It can be even more effective if you paraphrase by rewording their sentiments using your own language. By restating what you have heard, you are letting the speaker experience that they have been understood and that you are willing to suspend your own thoughts and focus on the speaker's view, concern, or idea. For example:

- "So, you are saying that you threw the ball when Susan said you were cheating."
- "Are you saying that you believe it would be best if we choose a leader for the project?"

Validate the speaker's statement. Let the speaker know that you see his or her point of view and that you can accept it as true *for him or her*. It does not mean that you agree with the speaker, only that you acknowledge the speaker's point of view. For example:

- "You seem very upset that Susan accused you of cheating. Have I got that right?"
- "You seem to believe that having one person run the group would be the most effective way for us to work. Is that correct?"

Empathize with the speaker. Express your understanding of how the speaker might be feeling—that you connect with the emotions that he or she might be experiencing. Again, it does not mean that you share the same reaction, only that you accept it as real for the speaker. For example:

- "I can imagine that you might feel hurt. That must be really frustrating."
- "I understand that you feel passionate about your view. Is that correct?"

Taking Perspective

The ability to take another person's perspective in a situation involves strong social intelligence and attention to a situation. This skill is very often challenging for students with ADHD who may appear to be rude and self-centered, but are lacking the strong cognitive skills needed to take another person's perspective. This struggle to "step into another person's shoes" might be seen in a conflict at recess with another student or in recognizing how their classroom behaviors are impacting the learning of others.

Having a strong ability to take another person's perspective contributes to greater empathy. Students with ADHD and executive function challenges benefit from direct instruction and practice in taking another person's perspective.

The following activities are intended to help students practice this skill. They will have to consider how someone outside of their situation is thinking and feeling. Students will learn to step outside of their own opinions and viewpoints and work to understand how someone in a different situation may be feeling or viewing a situation.

Taking Perspective with LEGOs®

• • •

The goal of this activity is to have students focus on how another student might view a situation, rather than how they themselves view it. To accomplish this, students will work to create the same LEGO® structure as a peer—*without looking at the peer's structure*. Rather, they will use the peer's verbal cues to try and imagine what the structure looks like. In working to recreate the peer's structure, students will have to think through the perspective of their peer and how that peer might view LEGO® pieces, shapes, etc.

Set Up:
- Divide LEGO® pieces into clusters of 10–20 pieces each, ensuring that each student in a pair will have the same number of pieces available to them.
- Consider intentionally pairing students with a peer that they may not know as well.
- Have students decide who will start as the builder and the copier.

Instructions:
1. Instruct the builder to create a small structure with the Lego® pieces in front of him or her, while the copier looks away.

2. Once the builder is done creating the structure, have the copier work to recreate the structure as closely as possible while following these rules:

   - No looking at the structure that the builder created.
   - The first partner can use any words to describe the pieces used and to explain the steps taken to create the structure.

3. Have the students switch roles so that the new copier has to work to gain the perspective of the new builder.

Discussion Questions:
1. What challenges did you and your partner come across while copying the builder's structure?

2. Were there any things that made it easier to copy the other person's structure?

3. What are some other situations where it might be helpful to be able to view a situation from another person's perspective?

What Are They Thinking?

· · ·

Now that your students have had some practice with taking the perspective of a peer, the following activity gives them a chance to get some more practice developing strong perspective-taking through thinking what others might be thinking.

Using the image on the following page, ask the students to consider how each character might be thinking and feeling in this situation.

You might want to have a conversation beforehand about what the students notice about the picture. For example, you can start by having students think about how they would feel if they were in the shoes of the boy playing video games. Then, ask students to think about how the other characters around the boy might be feeling. After having this discussion, ask the students to write down what the characters might be thinking in each thought bubble.

Optional Challenge Activity:

Once the students have filled in the thought bubbles for each character, have the students write a short play about this scene. Students can work with a partner or a small group for this activity as they work to consider how each character may perceive the same situation in a slightly different way.

What Are They Thinking?

. . .

The Art of Interrupting

There are appropriate, even necessary, reasons to interrupt someone when they are speaking. However, knowing when and how to appropriately interrupt someone who is speaking does not come naturally or easily for some students, particularly those who struggle with executive functioning challenges. Self-advocacy is a development skill. Some students and adults struggle with knowing when and how to speak up when necessary in various settings. Teaching students the following guidelines and techniques will help them take care of their own needs while respectfully attending to others involved in the conversation.

When is it okay to interrupt?

- **When there are emergencies or time issues:** Whether a bus is about to leave, or something dangerous or harmful is about to occur, it's essential to stop the current conversation and tend to the situation at hand.

- **When we feel overwhelmed:** If, as the listener, the student feels that there are too many things being discussed—or if the student is having trouble listening because he or she is focused on other thoughts—then allowing the speaker to believe that he or she is being heard serves nobody's needs. It's time to slow or stop the conversation and adjust.

- **When we feel confused:** If the student is doing his or her best to listen and understand, but is still not truly following what the speaker is saying, then the connection has been lost and it's important to stop and ask for clarity.

How can you appropriately interrupt?

- **Verbally**: Ideally, when there is a pause in the conversation, or when the speaker seems to have completed a thought or idea, then you can let that person know that you want to speak. You might say something such as, "Excuse me," "May I ask," or "I'm confused." If the person speaking still does not seem to be stopping, then you may need to interject another few words, but allow a few moments for the speaker to finish his or her thought and recognize you.

- **Nonverbally:** It is also possible to communicate a great deal by using our bodies. Just as you can let someone know that you understand or agree with what they are saying, you can also communicate confusion or disagreement by shaking your head or moving your arms. When you want to interrupt, you might use your hands by giving a small raise of your hand. If you are still unable to get the speaker's attention, you may need to very gently tap the person on the shoulder or arm.

COMMUNICATION GAMES

The following section contains additional games and activities that you can use to teach the rules of a conversation. In particular, these games give students a chance to practice positive communication skills and learn the importance of strong communication. Through fun activities, students start by learning the impact of using weaker communication skills and the potential problems that it can cause. Then, students gain practice in using strong listening skills while learning to communicate their ideas clearly to their peers. In addition, students will gain practice in understanding nonverbal communication skills that play a large role in how we communicate with others.

Telephone

· · ·

Have all the students sit in a circle where they can easily reach the person next to them. One person starts with a sentence and whispers it in the ear of the person sitting next to him or her. After listening to the sentence, the next person tries to whisper the same exact sentence to the next person.

This process continues until the last person in the circle is told the sentence, and then he or she says it aloud to the group. The goal of this game is to have everyone actively listen to each other so that the last person says the same exact sentence as the first person.

Why it helps: Playing this game helps students see that small misconceptions can end up making a huge difference in meaning. The students will learn the importance of active listening and have a glimpse of how rumors can start.

Emotion Charades

• • •

For this activity, make a stack of index cards with different emotions written or drawn on them. Students will take turns picking a card and acting out the emotion on the card without speaking. Then, other students will attempt to guess the emotion.

Why it helps: Reading facial expressions can be challenging for some students. This engaging game gives students a chance to practice reading the facial expressions of another person in a safe environment without potential consequences. It's important for students to be able to understand different facial expressions in order to pick up on what people around them are thinking or feeling.

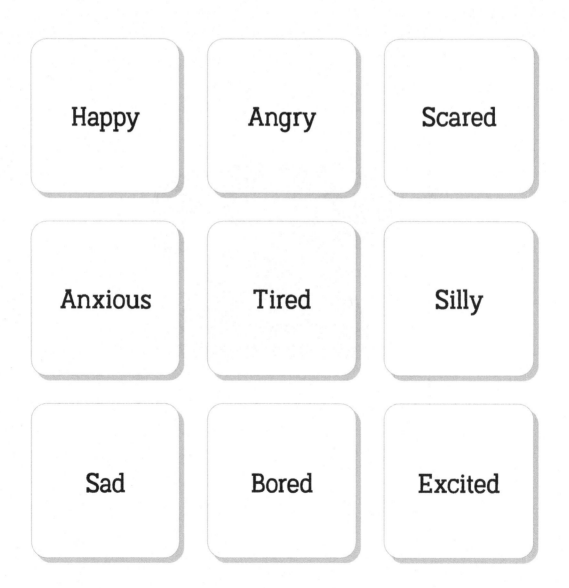

Happy	Angry	Scared
Anxious	Tired	Silly
Sad	Bored	Excited

Listen, Interpret, Draw

...

This activity gives all students a chance to draw while practicing their listening and inference skills. Students will be paired into Student A and Student B. Each pair should get a few pieces of paper and something to draw with. Student A starts by drawing a picture, while Student B looks away. Student B should neither look at the picture nor talk to Student A during this time.

After having a few minutes to draw, Student A describes to Student B exactly what he or she drew, while Student B attempts to copy the picture only from this description. Students can take turns being Student A and Student B. For a more challenging activity, students can only ask "yes" or "no" questions as they attempt to draw the same picture.

Why it helps: Through this activity, students must practice their active listening skills. Similar to the Taking Perspective with LEGO® activity, students also have to consider the perspective of the other student as they attempt to recreate the drawing only from their words. Students must also work to use language that clearly describes something in enough detail to someone who can't read their mind.

Finish the Story

• • •

In this activity, provide students with a verbal "story starter," and then give them a chance to finish the story. Your story starter should provide some context and setting, but leave it open for students to get creative. Then, students will add on to the story with one or two sentences at a time.

The story is "done" at any point when you or the students feels it has come to its conclusion. When more time allows, encourage the students to go into stronger detail in their story. You can also have students do this activity in pairs to practice communicating with each other. This activity can also be done with a familiar story, such as a nursery rhyme, but have students come up with a different ending.

Why it helps: Having students work to finish a story that another person presents to them challenges their ability to take the idea of another person and expand on it. For students who have a hard time letting others take control of a project or game, this activity is also a simple way to work on these skills.

Follow the Changing Leader

• • •

While students are sitting in a circle, choose one student to start as the leader of the group, while the remaining students are the followers. The job of the leader is to perform motions that the followers copy, such as clapping their hands or stomping their feet. The leader can also imitate facial expressions or perform other nonverbal movements.

At any point, the leader can switch to another student by a predetermined cue, such as winking or nodding, and then that new student takes over the leader's responsibilities. The other students have to figure out who the new leader is by focusing on nonverbal communication cues to imitate the new actions.

Why it helps: This game gives students a way to work on attending to nonverbal communication cues. By paying attention to facial cues and body language, students will practice focusing on others' gestures and emotions and learn how to use this information to respond accordingly.

TATTLING VS. REPORTING

Another difficulty that is often experienced by students with ADHD and executive functioning is understanding the difference between tattling and reporting. This can be particularly challenging for students with ADHD who are still working on developing strong communication skills. Understanding when a student is tattling compared to reporting requires strong emotion regulation skills, which we have also learned can be difficult for students with these challenges. Some students tend to be triggered strongly by what others might consider a smaller problem, which can lead to difficulties in knowing when they need to report a problem or when to let it go.

However, understanding the difference between tattling and reporting is an essential lesson for children to learn in order for them to understand when they should go to an adult for help and when they can let things go. Students are taught from a young age that it's not good to tattle on other students. Some students generalize this sentiment too broadly and fail to notify a teacher when they should. For example, if someone gets physically hurt, or is being intentionally bullied repeatedly by another student, these incidents should certainly be reported to an adult. If students feel uncomfortable telling the appropriate people about what they have witnessed or learned about, then they may attempt to handle the situation on their own in an inappropriate way (e.g., physically) or stay silent when it would be important for adults to have more information. By teaching students the difference between tattling and rightful reporting, teachers can significantly minimize this problem. At the same time, children also learn when they should let things go and when they should pay attention and work to solve a problem.

In order to help students learn the difference between tattling and reporting, it is helpful to first having an educational discussion regarding the difference between the two behaviors. **The following are some notes to guide your discussion:**

Tattling involves telling on another student for doing something that the tattler either finds annoying or thinks is wrong—*but for which no one is being hurt either physically or emotionally.* Tattling is often done with the intent of getting someone else in trouble. You are tattling if:

- The person being tattled on was not hurting anyone.
- The person did something by accident.
- The problem can easily be solved on your own.
- The purpose is to get someone else in trouble.

In contrast, **reporting** involves giving an adult information about a situation that will help keep that person or someone else safe. It is done with the intention of helping someone who is struggling or in danger of getting hurt. You are reporting if:

- The person's behavior is dangerous.
- The person did something mean on purpose.
- Adult help is needed to solve the problem.
- The purpose is to keep someone safe.

After guiding a discussion around what it means to tattle versus report the actions of another student, the following worksheet can be used to solidify students' understanding of these two behaviors. The worksheet asks students to cut, sort, and paste various statements into the appropriate "tattling" or "reporting" box.

Tattling vs. Reporting

· · ·

Look at the following statements and decide whether each statement is an example of tattling or reporting. Then, check statement in the appropriate "tattling" or "reporting" box.

Situation	Tattling	Reporting
He cut me in line.		
She called out without raising her hand!		
She fell off the playset at recess and is crying, and I think she might be hurt.		
He ran in the hallway.		
She tripped into me at lunch.		
They keep chasing me at recess, and I can't get them to stop. I really don't like it.		
She didn't finish her work before starting the fun activity.		
He's throwing rocks at other kids on the playground.		
The other kids won't let me play with them, and it's hurting my feelings.		
He's making fun of me and not listening when I tell him to stop.		
She Called …		

WITHOUT CALM, THERE IS NO LEARNING

When modeling and teaching communication skills to students, it's important to keep the following in mind: *Without calm, there is no learning.* So, whether you are teaching a student these skills independently or doing so in a group setting, do your best to *proactively* choose a planned time or plan to revisit a tough spot once the situation has calmed down for these teaching moments. The best teachable moment is not always during the event. In addition, if you have a student who is still struggling significantly despite your lessons and modeling, then you may want to consider seeking out the support of the school's speech-language pathologist. That person may be able to work more closely with the student to provide additional remediation.

THE VALUE OF CONNECTION

Although we have introduced a variety of activities and exercises that you can use to help students improve their communication skills, it can be challenging to teach students who do not feel confident, interested, or intrinsically motivated. Building a strong, personal, and warm connection with the student can help them push through and persevere. We all know the stories of the kid who talks about that "one special teacher" who made all the difference in helping that kid become the success he or she is today. The following are a few suggestions to help you create a close bond with the students who may be the hardest to reach.

Increasing Connection

- Greet each student by their name as they enter your space. This allows students to hear you say their name in a positive tone so they don't only hear it when being corrected.

- Make eye contact, perhaps even at their level, so that they feel noticed.

- Be discreet! When teachers need to provide support and guidance, kids often get embarrassed by this extra attention. Agreeing on private signals, passing notes, or asking the student for help as an excuse to have private time will allow them the discretion they may desire.

- Increase proximity: Whenever you are giving a student directions or corrections, ensure that you are in close physical proximity to that student, to the extent possible. That way, he or she can more easily pay attention to what you are saying.

- If a student is exhibiting challenging behaviors, use "I" statements to let the student know how his or her behaviors are impacting you. For example, "When you _____, I feel _____. Please _____." Using "I" statements reduces feelings of blame and makes it less likely that the student will get on the defensive.

- Don't dismiss or ignore the quiet ones. As discussed in Chapter 1, students who have ADHD and are more the "inattentive" type may appear to have everything under control. They may also be intelligent enough to compensate for the skills they lack to stay on task. However, they may be internalizing considerable struggles and doing their best to mask or avoid specific challenges, which increases their anxiety and/or depression.

- Find *something* to praise as much as possible. Kids who have ADHD and executive function challenges are redirected, corrected, and sometimes reprimanded all day long. In turn, their self-talk may be negative without others knowing. To balance out all the negative messages they receive, it's important to actively provide positive feedback not only for their accomplishments, but also anytime they exhibit positive behavior, maintain a good attitude, or put forth effort. However, some students view praise as a sign that they lack certain abilities and that their teacher thinks they need extra encouragement. Other students believe that a teacher's criticism, not praise, is a sign that their teacher believes they are capable. Therefore, when providing positive feedback, it's vital that your encouragement come across as very specific, genuine, and believable. Here is a three-word alliteration that we find helpful:

  ➢ **Notice** that your student is doing and/or feeling something positive.

  ➢ **Name** what you have noticed and the value in what you see.

  ➢ **Nurture** your student with warmth and appreciate them at the moment.

  For example:

  ➢ "Jarod, I see you are really working at that math problem. I notice you have tried a few times without quitting. That shows me you don't give up easily; good for you!"

  ➢ "Sara, I notice you are really trying, but I think maybe the strategies you are using or the strategies I am teaching aren't working for you. Would you like some help?"

- **Have your students complete the "Who Am I" worksheet that follows, preferably at the beginning of the school year.** The questions are intended to guide them in engaging in important self-exploration. It will also help you learn about their culture, their interests, their passions, their concerns, and their goals. By inviting them to share this information about themselves you are opening the door to connection.

Who Am I

• • •

As we begin this new school year together, I would like the opportunity to learn a little about you. Letting me know some things about you and your world can help me understand you and offer support and information that can be helpful in allowing you to be your best self. Below are a few questions. Don't overthink your answers, just put down your first thoughts.

Name _____

1. What are five things that are interesting or unique to your culture, religion, or heritage?

_____

_____

_____

_____

_____

2. What are your favorite things to talk about?

_____

_____

3. What name do you prefer to be called?

_____

4. How do you like to spend your free time? What are your interests, your passions?

_____

_____

5. What is the best book you have ever read? What did you like about it?

_____

_____

6. What is your favorite game to play? Why do you enjoy it so much?

_____

_____

7. Who is your favorite famous person and why?

_____

_____

8. What would make this school year feel and look like a success?

_____

_____

9. How can I best support you during the school year?

_____

_____

10. Is there anything else you would like me to know about you?

_____

_____

4. Collaboration: Working Together for Positive Change

DEALING WITH CHALLENGING BEHAVIORS: A DIFFERENT APPROACH

"What factor causes students to misbehave the most?" (We will reveal the answer at the end of the chapter.) The choices are:

- Lack of engagement
- Lack of coping skills
- Peer influence
- Bad parenting

This is a very important question to consider when working with students since our explanation of behavior guides our intervention. **In other words, we tend to intervene in situations based on the assumptions we have regarding why the behavior is happening.**

Students who struggle to follow directions, participate appropriately, and work independently when required can create a wide range of struggles and frustrations for the classroom teacher. In addition, when these are students who have an average or above average IQ—and have (at times) exhibited appropriate behavior—they may come across as lazy or unmotivated. It may even seem as if these students are seeking power and control instead of being respectful.

Conventional wisdom infers that if a student *wanted* to do what was needed and to behave appropriately, then that student could and would. This belief leads well-meaning adults to devise ways to help these students *want* to do what is expected. The most common approaches used to accomplish this goal involve offering rewards and introducing the threat of discipline or restriction. However, as many seasoned professionals have experienced, traditional behavior modification programs (e.g., sticker charts, reward programs, etc.) do not always work for kids who have ADHD and executive function challenges. Why? Well, as we explored in Chapter 1, the reward and motivation centers of the brain are under-stimulated among individuals with ADHD. Therefore, external rewards are often not stimulating enough to result in long-lasting changes in their behavior. When you add in the notion that for many of these kids, time is "now" and "not now," the idea of working toward a future reward doesn't necessarily motivate them in the moment. In addition, when you consider the impact of processing speed, working memory, internal/external distractions, and inherent difficulties in managing their emotions, it's easier to understand that, oftentimes, these students are not "lazy" or "unmotivated"—they genuinely lack the skills *in the moment* to do what is expected.

As adults, when we focus on changing or extinguishing a student's negative behaviors that are inappropriate in that moment, we risk sacrificing the opportunity to make lasting, durable changes. Perhaps more importantly we erode the connection and trust that is vital to help struggling students allow themselves to take positive risks. When we offer students rewards or threaten punishment—when they don't even have the skills needed *in that moment* to meet expectations—they may feel that we do not understand them, believe them, or trust them. This may cause a student to shut down and disengage, to fight back, or to have a meltdown, which only creates additional challenges.

A DIFFERENT VIEW

We have found that when we approach challenging students through a different lens—one that views challenging behaviors as caused by lagging skills and unsolved problems—we shift the whole dynamic of our relationship. As Dr. Ross Greene proposed in his groundbreaking book *The Explosive Child*, we must shift to believing that "kids do well IF they can." This viewpoint allows us to focus on understanding what is creating the problem for the student, what skills he or she needs to develop, and what problems need to be solved, so that the student can more consistently meet expectations.

Keep in mind that these students are not *choosing* to be difficult any more than one *chooses* to have a learning disability. They lack the skills needed to handle frustration, effectively solve problems, communicate their needs appropriately, and master situations that require flexibility and adaptability. The demands placed on them exceed their capacity to respond adaptively, and their response in certain situations is thus reasonable and appropriate given their circumstances. Therefore, for these students, their defiance (e.g., acting out or avoidance behaviors) is actually their **coping mechanism**. It allows them to avoid doing difficult tasks that they don't want to (or can't) do or to continue doing what they want to do—at least in the short term.

BUILDING SKILLS FOR SYSTEMIC CHANGE

The most effective way to help students learn to be more flexible, manage their frustration, and solve problems they encounter is to work with them to raise their awareness of the skills that they lack and, in turn, help them build these skills. This is accomplished by working with the student to brainstorm solutions to *actual* problems that arise in the classroom and by including students in the problem-solving process. While this process may seem obvious and simplistic, by using the following tips, you will begin to see true, positive change occur.

1. **Be a detective with the student.** When you see a student staring off into space, a student refusing to start his or her work, or a student who is annoying fellow classmates, rather than trying to *change* that student's behavior, step back a moment and consider *why* he or she is engaging in that behavior. Start from what you know about the student's profile. For example, consider what the student's executive functioning challenges are (e.g., ability to manage frustration, be flexible, etc.). Consider trying to figure out possible explanations as to why that student might be behaving that way even if he or she should not.

   You will want to include the student in your detective work. Very often, the problems that occur are consistent and predictable *because they are patterns of behavior*. Therefore, when possible, have a conversation with the student when the identified behavioral problem is not happening. It is always best to work proactively (or well after the challenging behavior has occurred) since we need to be *calm* so that the student is best able to engage his or her reasoning skills. Be sure to be discreet and let the student know that the conversation is private and safe. You may want to explicitly state that the student is not in trouble, but that you are trying to understand what is making it so challenging to meet the expectation at hand (e.g., working, being quiet, raising hand before speaking, etc.).

   You do not have to agree with the student's explanation for the behavior. Just make sure that you can really understand his or her perspective. At this point, you also don't want to offer any solutions or modify any expectations. Your goal here is to simply be a good listener: Ask whatever questions you need to understand the student's point of view and to express what you hear so that the student knows and feels that you truly understand his or her perspective and concerns. Even if the solution now seems obvious to you, resist offering it since we don't just want to solve current problems but, rather, to build skills that help the student generalize the problem-solving process to other situations.

2. **Share your concern and your perspective.** Kids can sometimes act in ways that seem as if they don't care about other people's perspective—that they somehow lack awareness or concern about how their actions impact others. Of course, we know that it's often not a lack of concern about others that drives their actions; rather, they are just so focused on their own perspective.

Therefore, an integral part of the problem-solving process involves sharing your concern and perspective, and perhaps that of others who are impacted by the behavior. Keep in mind that the student might not agree with your concern or perspective. However, it is still essential that the student be able to *understand* your perspective (and express this understanding to you) so that you are on the same page.

But here is the tricky part for some: What *is* your concern, and how can you best communicate it to the student? Is it a concern or just a preference? **The following handout contains an activity that may help you clarify your concern in a way that will make it easier and more impactful to communicate it to your student.**

Drilling Down Your Concern

• • •

1. Think about your concern regarding a student's behavior, and write down the reason **why** this behavior is a concern.

2. Next, ask yourself **why this "why" is a concern.** Write out your answer for clarity.

3. Now, do this a third time. **Why is this "why" a concern?** Each time you ask yourself this question, you are going deeper into understanding what is at the core of your concern.

4. In looking at this final "why," **what is your fear behind the "why"?** What is the BIG concern here?

5. Finally, write down your concern in a dynamic way that communicates your concern in manner that the student (and/or at least the parents) can understand.

The following is an example:

Behavior: You have a student who is pushing other students when he gets very upset.

1. He may hurt other students.

2. He may risk other students not wanting to be near him.

3. He may risk becoming isolated socially.

4. My fear is that he may start to believe that he is not likable and will start to feel bad about himself. This may cause him to withdraw and not be as willing to connect and learn with others around him.

5. "Sam, my concern is that you might be giving other children the impression that you don't want them to be friends with you and that they won't get to see the positive things that you have to offer."

3. **Invite the student to brainstorm solutions with you**. Now that you and the student have expressed your concerns and perspectives with each other, it's a good idea to state them both together. Ideally, you can have the student be the one to express this, but if he or she is unable or unwilling, you can. For example, "I wonder if there is a way to problem solve this so that I _____ (e.g., *still get to move around the classroom in order to help me pay attention*) and you _____ (e.g., *don't have to be concerned about me distracting others or destroying anything*)."

   During this brainstorming, be sure to write down any ideas that come to mind, even if, in your gut, you don't believe that a particular idea will be the ultimate solution. You want a flow of ideas that help the student develop problem-solving and reasoning skills. Let the student take the lead in offering suggestions since we all like our own ideas best! Once you feel that you have exhausted all possible ideas, evaluate which one will produce the greatest opportunity for a doable, durable solution to the problem.

4. **Accountability.** This fourth step is vital to the whole process because it provides a rubric by which to determine if the solution is working and what to do if it is not. Again, the value of this collaborative process is not just to solve the problem, but to teach the student effective problem-solving skills. Therefore, to address the implications of accountability before putting the solution into practice, make sure you have explicitly explored the following two questions:

   - *"How will we know that this solution is working?"* This question makes the student consider the desired outcomes of the solution. For example, "If I am using the fidget effectively, then I will be able to answer class questions, not distract others, and be more focused on my work."

   - *"What should we do if this solution is not working?"* Exploring this question *before* you implement the plan makes it less punitive if changes need to be made—because they have already been discussed and planned for. For example, "If using the fidget ball becomes too distracting or I throw it around without intentionally doing so, then I will go choose something else to fidget with."

5. **Plan a specific date to meet to evaluate if the plan is working**. This last step is vital and often overlooked. Often, students with challenging behaviors become used to believing that whenever an adult says, "Let's talk," it means they have done something wrong, disappointed someone, and are potentially in trouble. By choosing a specific time and date in the future to meet to evaluate the plan, the student knows that the meeting is not necessarily punitive. Even better, you and the student may have an opportunity to celebrate improved behavior—and the process of collaboration that led to the new solution. We want students to start to rely on using their words and engaging in structured conversations to deal with their challenges, as opposed to the behaviors they have used in the past.

   If, upon meeting, you find that the agreed upon plan is not working, that is okay! In fact, it's a new opportunity to learn what was missing from the first conversation. Perhaps there is now greater clarity regarding the concern and how it is impacting both you and the student. Or, perhaps the solution gave rise to a deeper concern. For example, now that the student is sitting more effectively and focused on his or her work, we see that the student's struggles are more related to the academic content than his or her behavior. We then need to explore new solutions and approaches.

COLLABORATIVE PROBLEM SOLVING IN ACTION

The section that follows provides some sample scenarios that illustrate this collaborative process in action. These scripts are *intentionally* overly verbose because they are intended to explain the process in greater detail. However, when you actually have these types of conversations with students, summarize your thinking and use minimal language. Using fewer words with students will allow them to hear you better, whereas being wordier can often increase stress and cause students to feel overwhelmed.

SCENARIO 1

Problem: Sam is talking out in class during group lessons. Parents of other students are starting to complain because their children are reporting that "one kid" is talking all the time.

Working Hypothesis: It feels like Sam is just trying to create disorder and distraction.

Already Tried:

- Giving him reminders to raise his hand
- Reminding him of his expected voice level (e.g., 0, 1, 2, 3) using a voice level chart
- Using a contingency plan (e.g., if you call out, then "you owe me time at recess")

New Approach: Collaborative Problem Solving

1. **Be a detective with the student.** It is likely that Sam will be resistant to this conversation at first. Especially before students are used to having collaborative problem-solving conversations, they will often be defensive or not yet see the value in sharing. You may also have to work together to figure out the "why" behind the behavior. Stick with it, and the more you practice this with your students, the more both of you will build this skill.

Teacher:	"I notice that, sometimes, when we are learning as group, you have a hard time keeping your voice down. What's up?"
Sam:	"I don't know."
Teacher:	"That's okay, let's figure this out together. Do you feel like you have a hard time keeping your voice quiet when it isn't your turn to talk?"
Sam:	"Yes."
Teacher:	"I wonder what could be making this challenging for you. If we can figure out why this is tough for you, I can help you make it better. Do you have any ideas why this is hard for you?"
Sam:	"I don't know, it's boring."
Teacher:	"What is boring?"
Sam:	"Sitting and listening is boring."
Teacher:	"Okay, so it sounds like when you have to sit and listen it feels boring. Thank you for sharing that with me. Let's figure out how to solve this problem."

2. **Share your concern and your perspective.** This part of the conversation intends to give the student a chance to hear *why* his or her behavior needs to change. However, be careful not to shame the student by making the student feel badly about what he or she has done wrong. Instead, commend the student for bravely sharing with you while acknowledging that there still needs to be a change. Be sure to connect your reason to the student.

Teacher:	"My concern is that when you speak out during group time, it makes it challenging for other students to learn. It can also make it hard for me to teach."

3. **Invite the student to brainstorm solutions with you.**

Teacher:	"I wonder what we can do to help you deal with your bored feelings in a way that will allow other students to continue learning. Do you have any ideas about how we can solve this problem?"
Sam:	"I'm not sure. Maybe I could build with LEGOs' or read a book while you're teaching."

Teacher:	"Hmm… My concern with that is that I would like you to be learning with us too. It's important that you participate and listen during these times. I hear that you might need some type of break during these times, though. How we can we have you here learning but help you get what you need?"
Sam:	"What if I took a break? It's a long time to sit and listen."
Teacher:	"I get that. I think a short break is a good idea to break up that time for you and get some of that extra energy you're feeling out. Let's come up with some reasonable break ideas together and decide how long they will be."

4. **Accountability.**

Teacher:	"It feels like we have a good plan in place. The last thing I am wondering is how we will know that our new plan is working?"
Sam:	"I think if I'm staying quiet and using the right voice level in class then we'll know that the breaks are working."
Teacher:	"I agree. Good work. I am here if you need me."

5. **Plan a specific date to meet to evaluate if the plan is working.**

SCENARIO 2

Problem: Adrianne does not start her math work in a timely manner. She tends to stare off into space, push papers around, or play with things in her desk.

Working Hypothesis: Adrianne finds it hard to stay focused on tasks that don't come easily to her.

Already Tried:

- Talking with her about the importance of starting assignments immediately so that she has enough time to complete them
- Asking her to clear off her desk so that she only has the one assignment to work on
- Encouraging her to stay on task by offering a reward if she finishes within the allotted time frame

New Approach: Collaborative Problem Solving

1. **Be a detective with the student.**

Teacher:	"I notice that when it's independent math time, you often don't get your work started. What's up?"
Adrianne:	"It's annoying, I just don't like doing it."
Teacher:	"I see, you find that doing the math is annoying. How so? Can you say more so I can understand?"
Adrianne:	"I just don't like doing it."
Teacher:	"Okay, can you tell me a bit about what you don't like about the math we are doing now?"
Adrianne:	"I didn't mind doing the adding and subtracting work, but these word problems are so confusing. I just don't get it. Why can't you just give us the math problems that we have to solve?"
Teacher:	"Oh, I understand, when you have to read through word problems, it gets confusing to you. And then you stop working."
Adrianne:	"Yeah, what's the point? I can't do them that way."

2. **Share your concern and your perspective.**

Teacher: "I understand that it can get frustrating when you are not sure what to do. My concern is that I want to be able to help you get passed the hard part. When you stop working, I don't always know why you have stopped."

3. **Invite the student to brainstorm solutions with you.**

Teacher: "I wonder if there is a way that you can let me know *why* you are not doing the work, and if we can come up with some ideas for what to do when the work is frustrating you."

Adrianne: "Can't I just skip those problems?"

Teacher: "Well, I suppose skipping them *would* be less frustrating. However, these types of math problems will come up in your real life—say, when you plan a party or want to cook. I want to help you know how to get passed the tricky part so you can figure out what you need to. So, what can you do when you are feeling stuck?"

Adrianne: "I can ask for help. But when I do, I forget what you say as soon as you walk away, and then I get stuck again."

Teacher: "Would it be helpful if I write down the steps as I say them, and then you can start the work?"

Adrianne: "Okay, I can try."

Teacher: "Great, and we can do this each time until you start to write those steps yourself. What do you think?"

Adrianne: "I guess that can work."

4. **Accountability.**

Teacher: "It feels like we have a good plan in place. The last thing I am wondering is how we will know that our new plan is working?"

Adrianne: "If I'm getting started right away on my math work and staying focused on it."

Teacher: "Great. Let me know if you have any questions to make this work."

5. **Plan a specific date to meet to evaluate if the plan is working.**

SUMMARY

Collaborative problem-solving conversations take practice for both you *and* the student. It takes practice for students to build trust and see purpose and value in sharing their concerns and perspective with you. Stick with it! They will learn to trust that speaking their truth is worth the effort.

When we focus on the triggers and underlying challenges that lead to behaviors, we can help students build skills that they can transfer to other situations. Remember, **students do well *if* they can**. If they truly cannot, then our challenge is to understand what is getting in the way and to help them build the skills needed to do things differently. This leads us to the following: What was the answer to the question we posed at the beginning of the chapter? **Lack of coping skills.**

5.
Stress Reduction For Students (and Teachers)

THE IMPACT OF STRESS

What are the greatest challenges that these professionals face in the classroom? With rare exception, the top answer I hear at training workshops is **stress**—both for professionals and their students. The teachers feel like they are not adequately prepared to meet their students' constant need for attention, supervision, and reminders to stay on task given their level of knowledge about ADHD, the added time it takes to work with these students, their lack of adequate classroom support, and their access to special education experts.

So, what do we do to help lower stress in the classroom? We first need to recognize the different ways that stress can manifest in each person so that we can appreciate it for what it really is. Often, we see behaviors in others that are off-putting, inappropriate, frustrating, and just plain confusing. Once we get a better understanding of how stress manifests (as well as its precursors), then we can effectively implement strategies that prevent its occurrence and alleviate its impact. In this chapter, we discuss the science behind the stress response and provide some activities to help students (and teachers) better manage the impact of stress in the classroom.

THE NEUROSCIENCE OF STRESS

When looking to enact some sort of change, we find that it's always helpful to understand the science behind *why* something happens. Therefore, when attempting to reduce stress in the classroom, it is helpful to discuss the neuroscience behind the stress response. Even for younger students, when we can give them a logical explanation that helps them understand *why* stress occurs, we have a better chance of partnering with them to affect change.

When teaching your students the neuroscience behind the stress response, you can either use the following graphic of the brain or draw a simple picture on your board. Rather than providing you with a diagram that describes all possible regions of the brain, the following graphic includes only three primary regions—the prefrontal cortex, hippocampus, and amygdala—given their central role in the stress response. There is no need to be precise regarding the placement or size of these different brain regions for your explanation to be impactful.

First, introduce the brain's **prefrontal cortex**, which is the area in the front of the brain located just behind our forehead. Talk about how the prefrontal cortex is the "thinking" part of the brain because it is where our executive functions are. It is the part of our brain that controls all of our mental processes. If you have already taught your students what the executive functions are (as described in Chapter 2), then you can just provide a brief review at this point.

Then, move on to a discussion of the middle part of the brain, which is known as the **hippocampus**. The hippocampus plays a critical role in our ability to form, organize, and store new memories. In other words, it is the part of the brain that helps everything we have learned "stick." It also is where we connect certain sensations (e.g.,

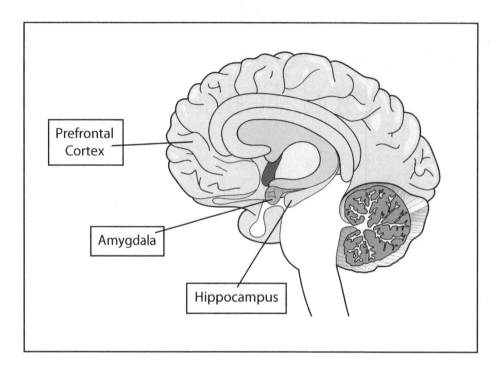

smell, sight, taste, sounds) with our emotions. For example, the hippocampus helps us remember where we were when we learned of certain news.

Lastly, introduce students to the back part of the brain: the **amygdala**. The amygdala plays a crucial role in processing emotions, such as fear, pleasure, and anger. When we experience intense emotions (e.g., fear, extreme sadness, anger, embarrassment), our bodies release a hormone called **cortisol**, which is known as the stress hormone. When this occurs, the thinking part of our brain (the prefrontal cortex) shuts down, and the reflexive, automatic responses of our amygdala turn on. This reaction activates what is known as the "fight, flight, or freeze" response.

When our "fight, flight, or freeze" response is activated, it becomes more difficult to engage in rational reasoning and decision-making. We have a hard time considering other people's perspectives, and we have a harder time accessing our memory. The brain just goes into survival mode.

Once students can understand the role that stress plays in impacting their ability to learn and solve problems, they can each benefit from having a variety of tools that can help them deal with stress and mitigate its negative effects.

The activities in the following section are designed to help students (both individually and on a class-wide basis) better understand their feelings, regain control of their emotions, and calm their bodies and minds. Exercises are also included to promote positive self-talk. Some activities contain written worksheets that you can simply give to the students, whereas in other activities, we encourage you to work interactively with the students. We recommend that you introduce a variety of activities and allow students to choose their own "best" way of releasing stress. **The overriding message is that while we may each experience and manage our emotions differently, we are each responsible for knowing how to best help ourselves.**

What happens when the Brain is in Survival Mode?

*Fight

*Flight

*Freeze

No learning can take place...
No problems can be solved...
Empathy for others becomes difficult...

The Fourth "F": Fib

Parents and educators are often surprised and frustrated when students tell lies, sometimes even very minor ones, rather than tell the truth. While we certainly need to address these lies, they are often caused by anxiety or lack of coping skills. For example, the student knows they are supposed to hand in a homework assignment that they didn't complete due to any number of challenges (too hard, didn't time manage properly, forgot materials, etc.). They don't want to fight, and they know they are being confronted with the question, but they are scared, embarassed, or ashamed to admit the truth. They don't want to say "it's too hard" or any other true statement and would rather risk getting caught than admit their truth in the moment.

A Note About Parents and Stress

Often, the stress that students experience at school is a reflection or an extension of what they experience at home. We have found that educating parents about the impact of stress on learning and behavior can help them recognize the value of reducing stress both for themselves and their children. **The handout that follows is intended to help students share what you are teaching them in class about stress and the brain with their parents.**

The Impact of Stress on Learning

• • •

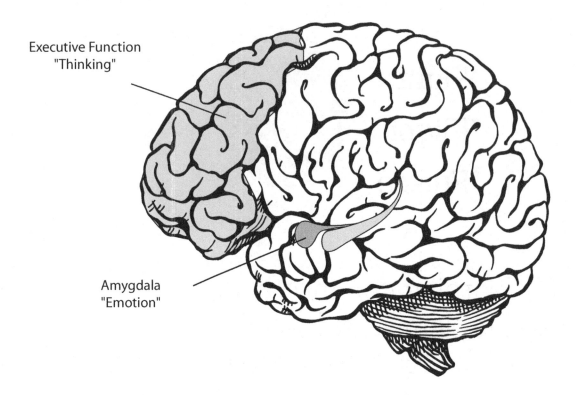

Executive Function
"Thinking"

Amygdala
"Emotion"

When we experience strong emotions (fear, extreme sadness, anger, embarrassment, etc.), our bodies release the hormone cortisol, known as the "stress hormone." This activates the rapid, reflexive responses of the amygdala (located at the back part of the brain), and the thinking part of our brain (the prefrontal cortex where the executive function are), shuts down. Reasoning and decision-making become challenging, we have a hard time considering other people's perspectives, and we have a harder time accessing our memory. The brain goes into survival mode, which is often experienced as fight, flight, or freeze.

Without calm:

- No learning can take place
- No problems can be solved
- Empathy for others becomes difficult

Calm is power! Stress is the gatekeeper to learning!

LANGUAGE OF EMOTIONS

Words can be very powerful. They inform how we feel and often shape how we respond to our challenges, to our opportunities, and to the other people in our lives. For example, if we tell ourselves that we are *anxious* about learning how to ride a bicycle, then that may lead us to act very differently than if we tell ourselves that we are *nervous*. If we are *anxious*, then we may be more resistant to asking for help, whereas if we are *nervous*, then we might feel more willing to accept guidance and support.

While we may agree on the essential definition of many words, when it comes to emotions, the words that we use to describe how we feel may communicate different meanings to different people. **We can help students learn about and play with different ways to describe various emotions. On the next page is an emotional word bank, which contains a list of emotions that are arranged in alphabetical order.** You may want to ask students to cut out words and put them in different piles that correspond with how they seem to describe similar moods or emotions. The number of piles and the number of words in each pile is not important, as long as students see that the words are related to one another in some way. Once they have created their piles, they can then glue each word group onto a piece of colored paper. They will then have a variety of ways to describe a similar emotional experience.

Emotional Word Bank

. . .

Accepted	Frightened	Overwhelmed
Amazed	Frustrated	Peaceful
Angry	Furious	Proud
Annoyed	Grieving	Rejected
Anxious	Guilty	Relieved
Ashamed	Happy	Resentful
Bitter	Hopeful	Respected
Bored	Hurt	Sad
Comfortable	Humiliated	Satisfied
Confused	Inadequate	Scared
Content	Inferior	Self-conscious
Courageous	Insecure	Sensitive
Depressed	Insignificant	Shocked
Determined	Inspired	Silly
Disdained	Irritated	Stupid
Disgusted	Jealous	Surprised
Disrespected	Joyful	Suspicious
Eager	Lonely	Tense
Embarrassed	Lost	Terrified
Energetic	Loving	Trapped
Envious	Miserable	Uncomfortable
Excited	Motivated	Worried
Fearful	Nervous	Worthless
Foolish	Optimistic	Zealous

EMOTIONAL THERMOMETER

Many times, the first step to helping our students regain control of their emotions is to assist them in understanding the value in regaining this control. The emotional thermometer is a great visual aid that students can use to visualize the importance of regulating their emotions. The goal of the emotional thermometer is to help students see the relationship between the feelings that they may experience and the consequence of allowing their emotions to dictate their behavior.

While you can just use the following completed chart to teach your students about the impact of emotions on behavior, we believe that the greatest value in this exercise comes from creating the chart with your students. **The handout on the following page provides guidelines to help your students create their own emotional thermometer.**

Emotion Thermometer

how you feel   **how you act**   **result**

how you feel	how you act	result
Furious Enraged Boiling Mad	Curse/Yell Become physical/ Shut Down	Can't reason/solve problems Risk punishment
Angry	Raise voice say angry things	Not able to listen Trouble thinking
Upset Annoyed Frustrated	Calmy express feelings, Act annoyed or upset	Can listen, speak appropriately Willing to compromise and reach solution
Calm	Happy Content	Productive Able to work with others

Without calm there is no learning and problem solving becomes difficult!

Handout

Emotional Thermometer

• • •

1. Begin with a blank chart, with only the thermometer present.

2. Next, write each category across the top ("How you feel," "How you act," and "Result").

3. Discuss the goal for behavior: being able to get along with others and do what is necessary or important in that moment. Write this goal in the lower, right-hand corner of the "Result" column (where we have written "Productive, Able to work with others").

4. Then, ask your students how they need to feel in order to be productive and work well with others. They can use a variety of words to describe these feelings. Write these words in the lower, left-hand corner of the "How you feel" column (where we have written "Calm").

5. Next, ask them how they generally act when they are feeling the way they have described. These words go on the bottom of the "How you act" column (where we have written "Happy, Content").

6. Once they have learned which feelings are necessary to be productive and work well with others, the next step is to move up the thermometer, beginning on the left-hand side in the "How you feel" column. What words might they use to describe the feeling they experience when they are slightly less than calm?

7. Use the emotional words they have chosen to ask them how they might notice if someone is feeling that way. How would that person act? Write their answer down in the "How you act" column.

8. Moving to the "Result" column, what is the likely outcome if someone acts as they have now described? How will this impact their ability to work, either by themselves or with others?

9. Repeat steps 6-8 two more times until you have reached the top of the thermometer.

You may want to use different colors to represent each different level of the thermometer. When the thermometer is complete, you may also want to hang a sample in the classroom. Next time you notice a student struggling to manage his or her emotions, you can gently encourage that student to reflect on what might happen as a result. Or, if you notice that a student is having trouble working productively, guide that student into reflecting on his or her "emotional temperature" to see what is needed in order to reduce the "fever." It might be time to take out one of the calming activities mentioned later in this chapter.

Emotional Thermometer

how you feel   **how you act**   **result**

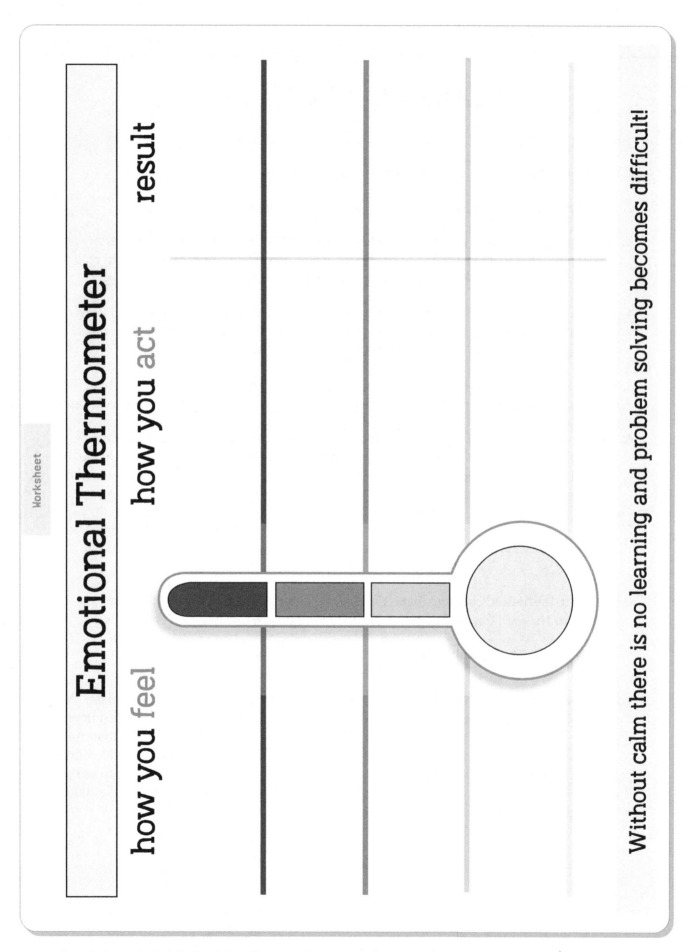

Without calm there is no learning and problem solving becomes difficult!

Worksheet

WHERE DO MY EMOTIONS HIDE OUT?

We each experience emotions differently. Sometimes, we feel our emotions as immediate pressure, and sometimes it's more of a gradual build up. Our emotions can also land in different parts of our bodies: our necks, our stomachs, our fists, etc.

The following activity helps students recognize the different ways that intense emotions may build up within their bodies. Using the diagram of the body below, help your students describe and visualize the physical sensations that they feel as they have different emotions or experiences. By combining these images with labels for their feelings, students can navigate their negative emotions and move to a more productive state of mind, where they can deal with and work through their stressors. **A handout with more specific guidelines for this activity is provided on the following page.**

Where Do My Emotions Hide?

• • •

1. Begin by discussing how our bodies sometimes have a physical reaction in response to different emotions. For example, certain emotions can cause us to feel tightness like a rubber band, a churning feeling like a spinning wheel, or a bubbling sensation like a volcano.

2. Help students use objects and colors to describe any intense feelings that they have experienced. In particular, ask them to name objects that are associated with certain feelings and where each object resides. For example, "When I am angry, it feels like a black rock in my stomach," or "When I am scared, it feels like a tight, orange rubber band around my shoulders."

   The following prompts can help them get started:

   • What type of object does the feeling feel like?

   • Where on their body do they experience the change?

   • What color describes the feeling?

3. Provide students with a variety of coloring instruments, and ask them to draw these objects and colors on the body. Doing so will allow them to express their emotions.

4. Finally, help the student think of three ways that they can discard the object from their body. For example, they can share their feelings with a parent, or put the feeling away in a box.

Where Do My Emotions Hide?

...

FUN WITH BREATHING

Breathing is something that we do all day long, usually without much thought or concern. What students may not realize is that our mind, body, and breath are all connected and influence one another. If you think about your breathing, notice how when you are angry or anxious, you breathe differently than when you are relaxed and calm. This change in breathing happens because when we experience stress, the body's "fight, flight, or freeze" response is triggered—which creates a burst of energy that makes your breathing faster.

One way to help manage our breathing is to practice deep breathing, which is also known as belly breathing or balloon breathing. Deep breathing involves engaging the diaphragm with each breath, so that the belly rises with each in breath and falls with each out breath. Deep breathing helps combat the stress response because it allows more oxygen to get into our lungs, which allows our muscles to relax and, in turn, can calm the mind.

The following three exercises contain breathing exercises that can help students become more intentional about their breathing. These tools will help them learn how to calm their whole bodies, as well as their minds. Calm minds make better decisions and are more able to learn, reason, and problem solve.

Breath Sequences

• • •

The following exercise is a fun way for students to practice breathing together. It can also be a fun way to let students be creative and take turns leading the activity. Have one student stand in front of the classroom to demonstrate and lead the class in a breathing exercise of their choice. They can choose from the following list of breath sequences or create their own original sequence.

The goal is to take between five and ten deep breaths: breathing in through the nose and out through the mouth. While doing the exercise, encourage students to let their bellies expand as they inhale, and to pull their stomachs in as they exhale.

Here are some examples of fun breath sequences:

Crocodile Breath

1. Crocodile breath: Inhale as you open your hands wide like a crocodile's mouth, and exhale as you close your hands back down.

Butterfly Breath

2. Butterfly breath: Inhale as you widen your hands like the wings of a butterfly, and exhale as you bring your arms together.

Rain Breath

3. Rain breath: Inhale as you put your arms up to the ceiling, and exhale as you gently bring your arms down and shake your fingers as if rain is falling.

Baseball Breath

4. Baseball breath: Inhale as you prepare to swing, and exhale as you swing your imaginary bat.

Spiderman Breath

5. Spiderman breath: Inhale as you prepare to spray the web, and exhale as you spray the web.

Blow Art

• • •

When we feel stressed, it can be hard to keep our body and breathing under control. We all know that feeling of intense overwhelm when our breathing starts to get faster and faster, we start to feel light-headed, and we certainly can't think our best. Although we may constantly tell our students to "take a deep breath," they sometimes need a bit more structure or silliness to get their breathing back under control. This craft is a great technique to structure the act of taking slow, deep breaths.

Materials:

- Large shoe box
- Thin or watered-down paint in a variety of colors
- Glitter
- Straws

Instructions:

1. Cut a hole just big enough to insert a straw into the narrow side of a shoebox.

2. Have your students choose a color and put some in the box near the hole.

3. Using the straw, tell your students to blow the paint to create different shapes or patterns.

4. If students want, they can add additional colors.

5. Encourage them to experiment with different kinds of breaths: short, long, quick, slow.

6. Once the paint dries, they can write a few sentences about what they notice about their painting.

Breath of Joy

• • •

Whenever you notice that students' attention may be waning—or when there is too much stress in the classroom or even too much movement—it's hard for effective learning to take place or for students to perform well. If students are sad or anxious, this can also interfere with their ability to engage. Whenever you notice that this is the case, it's time for a short burst of activity to wake the body up, get the blood flowing, and get the brain ready to work.

The breath of joy is one activity that you can use to help energize students and refocus their minds. To start the exercise, ask everyone to stand up and spread out. They will need enough room to move their arms fully to each side and be able to swing them fully to the front. Then, walk them through each of the following three steps. It is always helpful to demonstrate the three steps first before putting the exercise together.

1. Practice breathing in through the nose three consecutive times. Each of the three breaths should fill up the lungs only a third of the way. After taking three consecutive breaths, let out a big exhale through the mouth.

2. This time, with each breath in, move your arms in the following sequence:

   • On the first inhale, move your arms straight in front of your body.

   • On the second inhale, move your arms straight out to the side.

   • On the third inhale, move yours arms straight up to the sky.

3. Let out a big exhale through your mouth as you bend your whole body over and swing your arms down to the floor.

Repeat this sequence three to five times. Afterward, shake out your body and sit down. You should now all feel relaxed, energized, and ready to work.

MANAGING AND REDUCING STRESS

The following section contains exercises, worksheets that you can give directly to students and parents—as well as handouts that you can use with students—that provide them with a variety of options for managing and reducing stress.

Active Stress Release

• • •

This is a great exercise to do with the whole class to help everyone release any stress or tension that they may be feeling. Whether it is before a quiz or test, at the end of an instructional lesson, or in the morning before the start of class, this exercise helps to relax students' bodies and minds. In turn, they will be better able to focus and be present with you. The following is a script that you can use to guide students through this exercise.

1. Begin by sitting comfortably in your chair.

2. Gently close your eyes and relax your body so that the chair holds all of your weight.

3. Take a deep breath through your nose, hold it for a few seconds, and then exhale slowly through your mouth.

4. Each time you exhale, let your body release any tightness it may be feeling.

5. Now, I am going to ask you to tense and relax different parts of your body. As I go through each body part, tense the muscles in that area of your body as tightly as you can without straining. Hold the tension for seven seconds, and then abruptly release the tension, and let it fall away.

   • Squeeze your fist tightly as if you are squeezing an orange.

   • Shrug your shoulders as if you want them to touch your ears.

   • Scrunch your face as if you want to look *really* old.

   • Squeeze your belly in as if you are sucking all of the air out of your stomach.

   • Press your toes down as if you are pushing down the sand at the beach.

   • Finally, tense all of the muscles in your body at once, and then release. Imagine all of the tension leaving your body—leaving you relaxed.

   • Take two more deep breaths, and gently open your eyes.

6. If you notice that your students start giggling or smiling during the exercise, don't worry— you have accomplished your goal. They are now more relaxed, so they can engage the front part of their brain and tackle whatever is next.

Make a Calming Jar

· · ·

When students experience stress, they sometimes get overwhelmed or overstimulated to the point that it is impossible to engage with them. When this occurs, calming jars are a great sensory tool to help students refocus their mind and release any tension or stress they are experiencing. The calming jar uses visual input to help students self-regulate and get their emotions back in check.

Whenever students start feeling themselves getting frustrated, they can shake their jar really fast, which helps them release any pent-up tension in a non-destructive manner. Then, they can watch how long it takes for everything inside to settle down to the bottom, which helps relax their body and mind. They might even hum a beautiful melody in their head or imagine the sound of waves gently rolling to the shore.

Materials:

- Empty glass jar or plastic bottle
- Fine glitter
- Sequins or gems
- Hot water
- One bottle of glitter glue
- Hot glue gun or super glue

Instructions:

1. Have students fill an empty bottle about ¾ full of hot water. Hot water will help the glitter glue melt. Young students will need your help with this.

2. Then, ask students to squeeze in a full bottle of glitter glue into the bottle. More water will make the liquid move faster, and more glitter glue will make the liquid move slower.

3. Then, have students pour a small tube of fine glitter into the jar/bottle.

4. They can then add in any sequins or gems to the bottle, which will change the speed by which the objects in the bottle will fall.

5. Help students use a hot glue gun or super glue to permanently adhere the cap onto the jar or bottle.

6. Before students use their jars, make sure the cap is shut tightly, and wait for the glue to dry. Then, students are ready to shake their jars!

Journaling

. . .

When stress starts to overwhelm our brain, journaling can help us record our thoughts in a productive manner. By giving words to our feelings, we actually help calm the reaction of the amygdala and give our brain words that it can use to reason, problem solve, and calm down. Try one of the following journaling starters to get your thoughts flowing.

I am feeling _____ because _____

_____

_____

_____

Today has been a _____ day because _____

_____

_____

_____

I wish that _____

_____

_____

_____

Once you have written down some of your thoughts, see if you can answer these questions:

1. What is something I now realize about myself or the situation that I did not realize earlier?

_____

_____

2. What is one thing I can do now to help myself feel better?

_____

_____

3. Who would be a good person to help me if I want help with this situation?

_____

_____

Remind yourself: Your thoughts are only as powerful as you allow them to be. Through a lens of compassion and problem solving, you can very often reduce your stress and create a more positive outcome.

Doodling

• • •

Doodling is a helpful way to clear your mind and help you relax during stressful times. Doodling has been proven to calm the amygdala, the emotional regulator of our brain, and therefore helps to calm our mind and body. A doodle does not need to take on any recognizable shape. It can involve patterns, shapes, lines, or just random scribbles.

See what doodle you can create from the shape below. Allow yourself to be free of any expectations about what it should look like, and just let yourself experiment. Your doodle can be intricate or expansive—whatever your mind wants to create. After a few minutes, see if you can feel your body start to relax and if you are breathing more slowly and deeply.

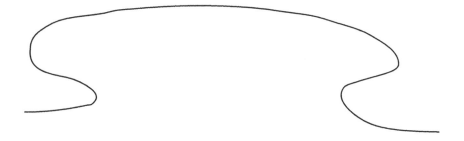

Repetitive Drawing

. . .

Drawing repetitive pictures helps to put your focus on something other than the thing that is creating your stress. Similar to doodling, repetitive drawing helps you de-stress because it calms our mind and forces it to focus on something simple and relaxing. Try out these drawing exercises to help get your mind off whatever is stressing you out and focus your mind on these fun drawings instead.

Draw 10 Tiny Trees

Draw 20 Stars

Draw 15 Birds

Draw 10 Suns

Make a Stress Ball

• • •

Stress balls are a great way for students to "squeeze" out their stress. Similar to the "Active Stress Release" activity, stress balls help release tension through the act of physically squeezing and then releasing the ball. As a bonus, they are also pretty simple and very fun to make. When introducing this activity to students, try filling the balloons with different materials and experiment with making them more or less full.

Materials:

- Balloons

- Filler (flour, rice, beans, etc.)

- Funnel

- Permanent marker

Instructions:

1. Have students stuff the spout of the funnel in the opening of the balloon.

2. Then, have them slowly fill the funnel with their filler of choice—making sure to fill it a little at a time. Younger students may need assistance with this.

3. Continually push the filler down inside the balloon to help stretch the balloon out.

4. If it starts to get a little stuck, simply shake the filler down the spout.

5. When the student's stress ball has reached its desired size, they can tie off and enjoy their new stress balloon.

6. If students want to add some character to their balloon, they can use a marker to give it a silly face and maybe some hair.

7. Once students finish making their stress ball, it can be helpful to associate feeling it with a positive statement about themselves. (See the "I am…" exercise in Chapter 6 for guidance on how to help students develop positive self-statements.)

When I Am Frustrated, I Can...

• • •

When we are feeling frustrated, or upset about the way things are going, it can get tough to keep our emotions in control. Frustrating situations will happen, but we can make them feel more manageable by having some strategies to help us manage our emotions. We call this "self-regulation." Look over the suggestions below and choose some strategies you like. There are also some blank boxes for you to add your own ideas. Mark in your top three favorite calming ideas. Next time you are feeling frustrated, you can refer back to these suggestions.

☐ Chew a Piece of Gum   ☐ Do Jumping Jacks

☐ Listen to Music   ☐ Use Playdough

☐ Take 10 Deep Breaths   ☐ Meditate

☐ Count to 10 Slowly   ☐ Draw a Picture

☐ Go for a Walk   ☐ Doodle

☐ Do Wall Push-Ups   ☐ Journal Your Thoughts

☐ Squeeze a Stress Ball   ☐ Close Your Eyes and Relax

☐ Use a Calming Jar   ☐ Think of Things that Make You Happy

☐   ☐

☐   ☐

☐   ☐

Put Yourself Together

· · ·

Do you ever feel completely out of sorts? When you just can't seem to calm yourself down, and you feel like you can't do anything that you are supposed to do? It can be tough to go from being very upset or angry to being calm and relaxed. Sometimes, we need a nice transition that gives us an opportunity to calm down the reactions of our amygdala and let the thinking part of our brain retake control. This is a great exercise to do with students when they need an opportunity to reset. The activity involves having students metaphorically put themselves back together as they put together a puzzle of themselves.

Materials:

- A photo (approximately 8 x 10) of the student when he or she is happy or doing something that he or she enjoys
- A piece of cardboard that is the same size as the photo
- Scissors
- Glue stick
- Small bag

Instructions:

1. Explore with students times when they may feel frustrated or angry to the point where they may not feel ready to do the work that is needed. During those times, students may need a few minutes to calm themselves down before they are prepared to start working again. Students may need to gather themselves, their thoughts, and their emotions; their physical body may need a chance to relax. In essence, students need some time to put themselves back together.

2. Have students glue a photo of themselves onto the cardboard.

3. Explore how students feel in this photo in order to elicit warm, happy, and relaxed emotions.

4. Instruct students to cut the picture into approximately 12 pieces. The pieces can be randomly shaped or more uniform.

5. Then, store the new puzzle pieces in the small bag.

6. Help students practice putting the puzzle back together again as you discuss what they can say to themselves when they are upset, frustrated, or angry. For example, "I will tell the teacher that I don't understand what to do," or "I will tell someone that I was hurt by what they said."

7. Let students know that next time they are struggling, they can take out their puzzle and take a few minutes to "put themselves back together" as they think about what they will do or say when they are done.

When Your Child Just Needs a Break

• • •

If it sometimes seems that your child is not working at his or her best, it may be that your child needs a break. However, the concern that many parents have is how they are going to make sure that their child gets back to work.

Experience and science have shown that our brains need time to rejuvenate after doing the same type of activity over an extended time. Helping your child know how to take **effective, limited breaks** can help him or her work more effectively and have more free time in the end. Here are a few suggestions to help you and your child determine the most productive way to manage break time:

1. During a time when you and your child are not involved in work activities, share with your child that you recognize that planning breaks in advance can help make work time more productive, which will also increase his or her free time.

2. Have a timer available to measure the passage of time and agree who will be responsible for setting and monitoring the device.

3. With your child, make a list of activities that can be done during five-minute and ten-minute breaks. Generally, these should be activities that can be set up and available in advance (so that prep time does not take away break time). These should be activities that can be easily completed during the break so as not to create the need, or temptation, to extend the break time.

Examples of breaks:

1. Assembling large puzzle that can stay out for an extended period of time

2. Shooting hoops

3. Playing a musical instrument

4. Reading a magazine

5. Talking on the phone

6. Taking a few turns on a board game

7. Doing push-ups, sit-ups, and other exercises

8. Drawing or coloring

9. Playing solitaire

10. Dancing to music

The Balancing Act

• • •

We are so focused on the negative things in our lives we don't always pay enough attention to what is going well. It is helpful to recognize that, even when we are faced with frustrations and disappointment, other areas of life bring us joy. Have your students look over the list of emotions from the "Emotional Word Bank" worksheet (p. 112). Encourage them to think about some of the emotions they felt during the past week, both the ones that made them happy and the ones that got them upset. Tell them to think about a range of experiences that they may have had in conjunction with these emotions, such as hanging out with friends, spending time with family, doing schoolwork, or participating in extracurricular activities.

Materials:

- Drawing of a balance scale
- Pen
- Paper
- Emotional Word Bank handout

Instructions:

1. Instruct students to write down some of the emotions they felt over the past week. Make sure they include at least two positive and two negative emotions.

2. Now, ask students to write each word in a different size, with the size of each word corresponding to how strongly they experienced that emotion. They may want to color the words in a shade that is representative of how it made them feel.

3. Finally, have students place these words on the scale. If the negative side of the scale is "heavier" than the positive side, help students think about what they can do to bring some balance into their life to add more joyful, relaxing activities.

The Balancing Act

...

6.
Helping Students Develop Grit

HELPING STUDENTS DEVELOP GRIT AND PERSEVERANCE

What makes some students more willing to persevere in the face of hard work? What makes some students more likely to try again even when they have failed? More importantly, how can we help those students who do not seem to persevere acquire the tools, patience, and courage to get back to their work again?

To address these important questions, we need to explore what underlies the challenges that some students (and adults) face in learning. For some, these challenges stem from difficulties with **motivation**. Some students just seem unmotivated to learn. Whether it is the specific subject being taught, or a lack of sufficient stimulation, they seem to shut down. Other students have difficulties managing **frustration** that interferes with their ability to work. These students get stuck—or even worse, give up—when faced with challenging situations. Lastly, some students struggle due to their **anxiety**. In particular, students can sometimes become so overwhelmed with negative thoughts that they are unable to proceed.

Have you ever had a student come up to you and say, "Teacher, my pencil broke," as they show you their tip-less pencil? Why doesn't the student take care of the situation independently? Whenever this question is posed to teachers, their explanation is often, "He has trouble problem solving." Although lack of problem-solving skills is part of the reasoning for some students, another explanation that is also important to consider: **Before learning can happen, we must *believe* that we have the ability to learn**. Many students, especially those who have those with ADHD and executive function challenges, may have not experienced the academic success that they may have felt they could or should have attained. While we have explored the many obstacles that some of these students face in learning, perhaps the greatest may be a growing pessimistic belief in themselves.

To help students believe they can learn, we must address the following questions:

1. What is their *mindset*? In other words, what is their belief about their ability to learn and face challenges? What is the story they tell themselves when they are faced with a challenge? What is their self-talk? What are the messages that they receive from those around them about their abilities?
2. How can we help students develop grit and perseverance when they face their greatest challenges?

Before we can explore how to help students believe that they *can* learn and persevere, let's start by understanding how our beliefs and outlook *impact* our motivation and willingness to face challenges.

WHAT IS YOUR MINDSET?

You may be familiar with the groundbreaking work of Dr. Carol Dweck on how our *mindset* impacts our motivation and our productivity. In this section, we summarize the findings of her work and help you teach the essential concepts to your students (and their parents).

In perhaps one of her most famous studies, Dweck asked seventh grade students to complete a test involving a relatively easy set of puzzles. The students completed the puzzles independently, in a classroom away from their peers. When students finished the puzzles, they were given differential feedback about their performance. Half of the students were told, "You must be smart at this," and the other half were told, "You must have really worked hard." After receiving this feedback, each student was presented with a series of follow-up tests and given a choice about which test they wanted to complete. One test was described as difficult and challenging in nature, and the other was described as easy—much like the puzzles they had just completed. Interestingly, 90% of students who were told, "You must have worked really hard" chose the more difficult set of puzzles, whereas students who were told that they were "smart" chose the easier option.

Why did this happen? It was the effects of the differential praise. Students who were told, "You must be smart at this" were praised for their **intelligence**. As a result, they wanted to focus their energy on looking "smart." Therefore, when the puzzles became more challenging, they began to doubt their intelligence and, in turn, gave up. As the puzzles became more difficult, they showed lower levels of confidence, motivation, and performance. They were also more likely to lie about how they did to their peers. In contrast, the students who were told, "You must have really worked hard" were praised for their **effort**. As a result, these students focused their energy on actually learning how to complete the puzzles. Because they were praised for trying, *they kept trying*. In turn, their level of confidence, motivation, and performance increased relative to students in the other group.

From this research, Dweck and her team established the following terms to describe people's beliefs in their ability to learn and face challenges: *fixed mindset* and *growth mindset*. Those who have a **fixed mindset** believe that intelligence and expertise are based on fixed, unchangeable traits. That is, some people are smart, and some people are not. They view effort as fruitless because people either "get it" or they don't. They avoid challenges, give up easily, and use negative self-talk. When others talk about their accomplishments, it may feel threatening or judgmental.

In contrast, those who have a **growth mindset** believe that intelligence and expertise can be developed over time. They demonstrate a desire to learn, and they recognize that brain and talent are just the starting points—effort, strategy, and instruction are the pathway to mastery. They embrace challenges, persevere, and use motivating self-talk. They view the success of others and criticism as inspirational and helpful feedback.

In order to help students develop a growth mindset, we need to help them *experience* that they *can* actually succeed. Therefore, when giving praise to students, it is important to praise their efforts as opposed to their perceived intelligence. When we tell students how good they are at something or how smart they are, this can sometimes cause them to fear trying a task altogether because they are worried about failing and not living up to the praise. In contrast, praising students for their efforts encourages them to work harder. Therefore, give praise when students are putting forth effort, using their skills, and sticking with something—even when the work is hard for them or they are not feeling their best. **The following are some examples of praise that encourage the development of a growth mindset:**

- "You tried really hard on that."
- "You must be focusing on the ball. Keep working on your skills in the batting cage."
- "I know this is really challenging. I like how hard you are working."
- "You found a good way to do it. Can you think of other ways that may also work?"
- "You came up with a really good strategy for the problem."
- "Your determination to stick with your plan really made a difference."
- "I'm really proud of the way you didn't give up and kept fighting despite the setbacks."
- "That was a long assignment, but you stuck with it and got it done. That's great."
- "I like the effort you put in. Let's work together some more and figure out what you don't understand."

Carol Dweck also emphasizes the importance of teaching students about how learning happens. She found that students showed a significant improvement in their grades when they were taught that every time they push themselves out of their comfort zone to learn new and difficult things, the neurons in their brain form new, stronger connections. **The following exercise will give your students a demonstration to visualize how this learning process happens.**

The Neurons That Fire Together Wire Together

• • •

Inside your brain are billions of cells called neurons. Neurons are a special type of cell that transmits information throughout the body. As you see below, each neuron has dendrites and axons. The dendrites bring the information to the neuron, and the axons take the information away from the cell body. The information from one neuron flows to another neuron across a space called a synapse.

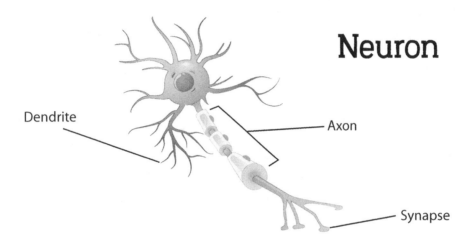

Every time you learn something new, your neurons form new connections with one another, which physically changes your brain. This is known as **neuroplasticity**. There is an expression that says "**The neurons that fire together, wire together**." This means that the more you **practice** and **review** what you learn, the stronger these neuron connections become. The more connections, the stronger your memory is for that information.

Materials:

- Chenille Stems (Pipe Cleaners)
- String
- Scissors

Instructions:

Making the Neurons

Each student will be making their own neuron out of pipe cleaners as they learn about the different parts of a neuron.

1. **Axon:** Sends information away from the cell body
   - Use one pipe cleaner to create a long axon, folding it over to leave room for the synaptic terminal.

2. **Synaptic Terminal:** Sends information to other neurons
   - Using the one end of the axon, make two branches for the synaptic terminal.
3. **Cell Body:** Supports the function of the neuron
   - Wind a pipe cleaner into a ball and use an end to attach it to the axon (the other side from the synaptic terminal).
4. **Dendrites:** Tree-like parts that receive information from other neurons
   - Use one or two more pipe cleaners to make various branches and attach to the cell body.

Teaching About Neural Connections

To demonstrate the concept that "neurons that fire together, wire together," students will be building strong connections with a partner's neuron.

1. Give each student about 10 pieces of string, approximately six inches each.

2. Have students pair up and stand across from each other, holding the neuron they made and their pieces of string.

3. Give students an age-appropriate, but very challenging fact or quote, to memorize with their partner.

   - Examples: a vocabulary word from a science unit, a phonics rule, a math fact, or the role of a part of the brain/neuron

4. Each time one person in the pair says the fact, they tie the string on their neuron and pass the other end to their partner to do the same. The string should be tied from one teammate's dendrite to the other's synaptic terminal.

5. Keep going until both students have memorized the fact.

   - To make your point further, tell your students that you are going to try to cut the connection with scissors when they only have a handful of connections. They will see that you can cut through the connection because it's still pretty week, just as the fact is in their brain.

   - Once students have built up many connections, try to cut their connection again. This time, the buildup of strings will make it too hard to cut through, as the neural connection is strong and the fact is on its way to being memorized.

6. When they are done, have students notice how thick the string is and imagine these connections being made in their brain between their own neurons each time they practice and review information.

The more you practice, the stronger the connection gets,
and the more you can improve.
The neurons that fire together wire together!

SELF-TALK AND GROWTH MINDSET

It is important to realize that many people have some specific areas where they have developed a fixed mindset. For example, Cindy grew up believing that she was not artistic or athletic. Carly believed that she could never move across the country by herself and start a career in a state where she didn't know anyone. We will share with you our own growth mindset journeys at the end of this chapter, but we first want to discuss how the concept of self-talk is associated with growth mindset.

Self-talk is the voice in our head that guides our emotions and our behaviors. The language that we use and the language that our students use has a true impact on the mindset that we truly believe and practice. Paying attention to the language that we use—and understanding the meaning behind it—is a great way to foster a growth mindset. It helps us believe that we are always capable of growth and improvement. **The following exercises highlight the power of self-talk and the "story" that we tell ourselves.**

Stuck on an Escalator: Addressing Mindset

* * *

The following activity is intended to demonstrate how our mindset impacts our actions. Through this activity, you can facilitate a discussion about students' perspectives about their own mindset.

1. Show your students the "Stuck on an Escalator" video, which you can easily find on YouTube (http://bit.ly/PTstuckonescalator).

2. In this video, two people are riding an escalator when it suddenly stops. They both respond by standing in place, calling for help, and lamenting their situation as unsolvable.

3. Ask your students to answer the following questions:

   • What would you do in that situation?

   • Why do you believe the adults responded as they did?

4. Have students pair up with one or two other students and discuss their answers for two to three minutes.

5. Discuss as a class what their thoughts are. This conversation will highlight the power of self-talk and the "story" that we tell ourselves.

6. Now, ask students to independently think of a time when they felt "stuck on an escalator" and what their self-talk was in this situation. Are there any messages they can recall being given by other people that contributed to a negative belief in their ability to "walk off" the escalator themselves?

The Power of Using Self-Talk as Guidance

. . .

The following exercise incorporates the concept of a growth mindset and the development of grit. The objective of this exercise is to help students explore their internal conversation and how it impacts their motivation, effort, grit, and performance. You will be asking your students to complete challenging activities that require patience and perseverance. Then, you will help students reflect on what they noticed about their own mindset and their willingness to stick with work they find frustrating and difficult.

Before starting this activity, it is essential that students know with 100% certainty that they will NOT be evaluated on any aspect of the activity. Let them know that you are aware that the activity will be extremely challenging and possibly too difficult for them to achieve at first. Discuss with students that the purpose of doing the activity is to help them see how they respond to challenges and what they can do to deal with whatever frustrations, doubts, or difficulties arise. The goal of the activity is to help them develop strategies for staying connected to their goals in the face of obstacles.

Provide a variety of age-appropriate, challenging activities that require different types of skills (e.g., rebus puzzles, word hunts, memorizing famous quotes, toothpick puzzles, tavern puzzles, etc.). We have included toothpick puzzles on the following page as an example.

Then, have students consider the following questions as they are completing the activity. During the activities, monitor the students and jot down some phrases that you hear from them to guide the next discussion. You may want to have students work individually or as pairs.

Questions to consider:

- Before the activity:

    1. What is your mindset as you begin this activity?

    2. Does the activity remind you of anything you have done in the past?

    3. What part do you think will be the most challenging?

    4. What can you do if it gets challenging so that you can keep learning and persevering?

- During the activity:

    1. What are you saying to yourself as you work?

    2. What part is going well for you?

    3. What part is challenging?

    4. What do you need to help you? Information? Practice? A new strategy?

    5. What have you done in the past that has helped you with this kind of challenge?

- After the activity:

    1. How did you stretch yourself during this challenge?

    2. What did you learn about yourself?

    3. How can you use this knowledge in the future?

Toothpick Puzzles

• • •

Instructions:

Below are three diagrams.

1. Lay out the toothpicks in the pattern you see on the paper.

2. Remove the number of toothpicks indicated to solve the puzzle.

Puzzle 1: Remove one toothpick to leave three squares.

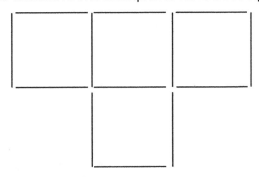

Puzzle 2: Remove three toothpicks to leave three squares.

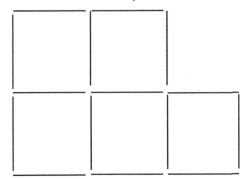

Puzzle 3: Remove six toothpicks to leave two squares.

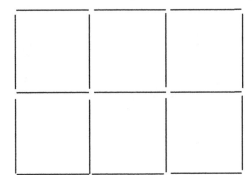

Answers to Toothpick Puzzles

...

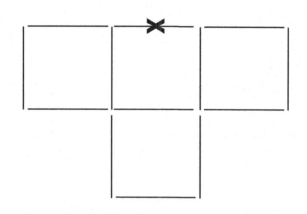

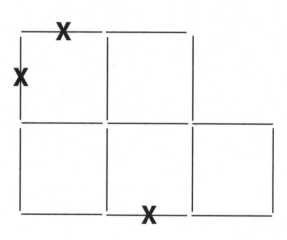

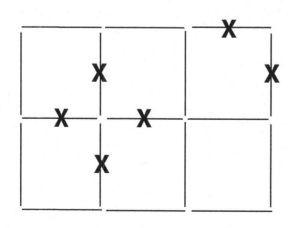

Two Wolves

• • •

Our thoughts become our words, and our words have a powerful influence on our beliefs about ourselves. What is the story that your students are telling themselves? If they are filling their heads with negative thoughts about themselves, then chances are they are feeling sad, anxious, or stressed.

Although we can help students see the positives about themselves while we are with them, when we are not with them, it is vital that they continue being able to give themselves positive messages. We want to raise their awareness of their self-talk with regard to their beliefs about themselves.

One way to begin teaching students about the power of their words is to introduce them to the Cherokee parable about two wolves:

Two Wolves

An old Cherokee was teaching his grandson about life.
"A fight is going on inside me," he said to the boy.

"It is a terrible fight, and it is between two wolves.
One is evil—he is anger, envy, sorrow, regret, greed, arrogance, self-pity, guilt, resentment, inferiority, lies, false pride, superiority, and ego."

He continued, "The other is good—he is joy, peace, love, hope, serenity, humility, kindness, benevolence, empathy, generosity, truth, compassion, and faith.
The same fight is going on inside you—and inside every other person, too."

The grandson thought about it for a minute and then asked his grandfather,
"Which wolf will win?"

The old Cherokee simply replied, "The one you feed."

After reading through the parable with your students, discuss how the story illustrates the battle that we all experience between positive and negative thoughts. When we feed our negative thoughts, we feel less confident in our ability to persevere and use our strengths and resources to face our challenges. Remind your students that "What you pay attention to grows." The next exercise, "I am…" will help students nourish their positive thoughts and beliefs about themselves.

"I Am..."

• • •

Sometimes, the positive messages we tell ourselves are things that we currently believe and trust to be true. However, it can also be helpful to use self-talk that reflects something we would *like* to be true about ourselves. The trick is to say that statement in the present tense as if it is already a reality. This is known as an affirmation.

In this activity, you will help your students develop a deck of affirmation cards that they can review every day. The deck should include some statements that they feel already represent their strengths or beliefs, and some that reflect desires or perspectives that they are working on. For example: "I can do hard things," "My mistakes help me improve," and "My hard work helps my brain get stronger."

Once students have created their deck, encourage them to read their affirmations every day; they can do so each morning, after lunch or at some other transitional point during the day. You might even suggest that they make a second deck that they can keep at home.

Materials:

- Three inch by five inch index cards with a hole punched on the top left, six per student
- Binder ring for each student
- Colored pencils

Instructions:

1. Give each student six index cards to begin their stack.

2. Explain to students that, "What you pay attention to is what grows." The words that they use to describe themselves have the power to shape their confidence. You can also reference back to the "Two Wolves" exercise to reinforce this concept to students.

3. Using different colored pencils, ask students to write down three positive statements about themselves that they believe to be true, one on each card.

4. Next, ask them to write down three statements about themselves that they *want* to be true, or that they at least want to be true more often. These are the things they are working on.

5. Mix the deck so that the cards are interspersed, and then connect them together using the binder ring.

6. Help students choose a time of day when they will read their affirmation cards so they get into the habit of hearing positive messages.

Incorporating Parents in Building Growth Mindset

In helping your students develop a growth mindset mentality, it is very important that the messages they receive from you are reflective of the messages they receive at home. Parents sometimes focus more on their children's grades as a measure of their success, without knowing the bigger picture of how to best support them.

The "What's Your Mindset?" handout is intended to give parents a basic understanding of the concept, as well as provide them with examples of growth mindset language they can use in communicating with their children.

What's Your Mindset?

...

We know that some students struggle to keep themselves motivated when work gets challenging. In fact, many adults do too! In addition to focusing on teaching academic curriculum to your children, our goal is to improve their motivation to learn and their willingness to face learning challenges.

As teachers, we are actively talking to students about how they learn and about different strategies they can use when they may be feeling frustrated, stuck, or discouraged. We are sharing this approach with you so that you may consider using this with your child at home and supporting the work we are doing with them at school.

Mindset for Learning and Performing

A student's response to challenges arises from the beliefs the student has about their intelligence. In fact, before learning can happen, we must believe that we have the ability to learn! Otherwise, we don't attempt to try to solve problems on our own.

To help students learn to persevere, one of the approaches we take focuses on something called "mindset." This evidence-based approach identifies two different "mindsets" for learning: **fixed** and **growth**.

In a **fixed** mindset, people believe that their basic qualities, like their intelligence or talent, are fixed. You either are or aren't good at something, because it's just who you are. You may notice in your own lives the people who give up before they even try, such as when the box comes with a new toy or piece of furniture to build and someone says, "I can't build—you do it." Or when there is a problem with their cell phone and they pass it off to someone for help without even attempting to troubleshoot themselves. They are working from a "fixed mindset" perspective.

In a **growth** mindset, people believe that their abilities can be developed through hard work—they can become better at something by putting in the effort to learn and practice. You can see lots of examples of people who are willing to believe they can get better at a challenging activity by watching shows like *Dancing with the Stars* or *Biggest Loser*. These people all take on a challenge, which requires overcoming previous assumptions about what they can and cannot do.

Helping your children develop a growth mindset, a belief that they can become smarter or better at something, creates a love of learning and a willingness to keep going even when work is hard and they experience failure. You may want to watch this video about famous people who were not always the success we know them to be today: *bit.ly/PTSfamousfailures*. It's very inspiring!

How can we help students develop a growth mindset?

1. In class, we taught students how learning happens in the brain. Ask them to show you and to tell you what "The neurons that fire together, wire together" means.

2. When your children are feeling stressed or anxious, it is more difficult to learn. We taught them strategies to calm their brains so that they are more ready and able to learn. Ask them what strategies work best for them and request that they help you learn some strategies for yourself as well.

3. Praise with positive impact. We often believe that we are doing the right thing by telling our children how good they are at something or how smart they are. Researchers have discovered a surprise, however. They found that sometimes this causes children to have a fear of trying, thinking that if they try, they may fail and not live up to the praise. On the other hand, they learned that praising their efforts encourages children to work harder.

When praising your children, see if you can notice your children's efforts when they use strategies and when they stick with something, even when the work is hard for them or they are not feeling at their best. Comment about what you notice, and try to be specific about what you are praising. Doing so will cause them to pay attention to the things they can control (effort), rather than simply the end result, which may not be an accurate representation of their knowledge or skill. This will encourage them to keep trying to improve.

Here are some examples of growth mindset praise:

- "You tried really hard on that."
- "You must be focusing on the ball. Keep working on your skills in the batting cage."
- "I know this is really challenging. I like how hard you are working."
- "You found a good way to do it. Can you think of other ways that may also work?"
- "You came up with a really good strategy for the problem."
- "Your determination to stick with your plan really made a difference."
- "I'm really proud of the way you didn't give up and kept fighting despite the setbacks."
- "That was a long assignment, but you stuck to it and got it done. That's great."
- "I like the effort you put in. Let's work together some more and figure out what you don't understand."

Help children give themselves positive messages:

When they say...	Help them say...
I'm never going to get this.	What should I try instead?
I just can't do this!	I'm going to have to practice this.
This is just too hard!	This is going to take some time.
It's easy for her—she's smart.	I'm going to work out how she's able to do this.
My answer is fine the way it is.	What can I do to make my answer even better?

Building Confidence to Build Growth Mindset

Sometimes, we need to build back some lost confidence by helping students recall and appreciate past experiences when they were successful. **The following worksheet can help your students appreciate the efforts and process that have gone into past achievements.** It may be helpful for them to complete this worksheet with the assistance and input of a parent who can help them look back on previous accomplishments that they may not recall. For example, the parent may be able to remind them of a time when they first learned to ride a bicycle, asked a stranger a question, memorized information, or read challenging words. The size of the accomplishment is not what is important; it's recalling that they didn't give up and can now remember it as an achievement.

I Did It!

• • •

Each time you face a challenge—whether in school, during extracurricular activities, socially, or otherwise—it's not unusual for your inner voice to wonder if you will be able to succeed. That conversation inside your head is actually where the process of achievement begins. So, how do we know if we can do something? One way is to call upon past experiences and learn from *how* we were able to conquer the things that we have already done.

Think of three things that you've accomplished in the past—things that may seem easy now, but were new and challenging experiences at the time. You may not even remember how you learned what you know now, so you may want to ask your parents what they can tell you about when and how you learned.

1. My accomplishments
   • _____
   • _____
   • _____

2. What made them so challenging? _____
   _____

3. What did I tell myself as I was trying? _____
   _____

4. What strategies did I use? _____
   _____

5. How long did it take to master these challenges? _____
   _____

6. Did anyone help me? _____
   _____

7. What did I learn about myself that feels great? _____
   _____

8. What strengths and talents do I have now that I can use for other challenges? _____
   _____

BECOMING "GRITTY"

When people hear the word *grit*, they sometimes think about coarse sand or stone, or perhaps cornmeal. However, these days, people increasingly think about the definition of grit as having to do with character: courage, backbone, spirit, strength of will, nerve, toughness, resolve, resolution, determination, tenacity, perseverance, and endurance. **Along with developing a growth mindset, helping students develop grit is perhaps one of the most important ways to ensure their academic success and more.**

For students who struggle in school—whether it's because of ADHD, executive functioning challenges, learning difficulties, or other reasons—helping them stay engaged with their work and not quit is the greatest challenge of all. **It's like they feel stuck in the mud and cannot get out.** While we certainly want our students to have a growth mindset, they will not gain any traction to get out of the mud if they don't stay with the work when it gets hard. That is where being "gritty" becomes so important. When students experience themselves improving at a given skill as a result of sticking with a difficult task, this experience can provide them with the feeling that they *can* have more control over the outcome.

In fostering a growth mindset and practicing "gritty" behaviors, we need to help our students reframe their "can't" into "can't yet"—and, even better, into goals. We all have things that we feel like we simply aren't good at, but the key in having a growth mindset is genuinely believing that we *can* get there. It will just take some grit!

On the following pages are two worksheets that you can give students to complete independently to help them get into the habit of becoming "gritty" in the face of challenges. Remember: We *can* do hard things.

Draw the Meaning

• • •

Instructions:

The following are some quotes that demonstrate a growth mindset. Growth mindset is the belief that we are all capable of growth and change. By changing the words that we use about ourselves, we can start to believe and practice this mindset. Below each quote there is an empty box where you will be drawing a picture of what the quote means to you.

"Mistakes help me to improve."

"I'm going to use the strategies I learned to get through this challenging work."

"It's okay not to know; it's not okay not to try."

"Believe that you can, and you are halfway there." — Theodor Roosevelt

"I can do hard things."

I Can't... Yet

• • •

Use this worksheet to think through some of the things that you want to improve on—things that you feel like you can't do, but that you want to improve at. By helping reframe your language, you can practice reframing your "can'ts" into goals.

I am good at...

1. _____

2. _____

3. _____

I wish I was good at...

1. _____

2. _____

3. _____

I will work toward these goals by...

1. _____

2. _____

3. _____

You can be good at these things too. It just takes some time and effort to get there!

Deliberate Practice

Psychologist Angela Duckworth (author of *Grit: The Power of Passion and Perseverance*) has done a tremendous amount of research to see what we can learn from "gritty" people and how to help others develop grit. One of the essential takeaways from her work is the importance of **deliberate practice** as a way to persevere toward your stated goals. Deliberate practice involves:

1. **Making a specific, detailed plan**: Write out the steps that you will take to reach the goal.

2. **Using positive self-talk**: This can include a script of positive mantras or statements to help with perseverance.

3. **Setting an intentional focus**: Proactively block out things that may cause a distraction (e.g., phones, friends, television, hunger, etc.).

4. **Actively seeking feedback**: Receiving objective input regarding your progress is a valuable tool to help you stay on track.

5. **Reflecting and adjusting**: Grit is not just about staying with the plan; it's about knowing when and how to refine your strategy if you are not achieving your desired results. It involves asking yourself *why* you are not where you thought you'd be. Does the plan still make sense? Is support needed?

Too often, we jump into our work without taking a moment to make a plan to improve our odds of a successful outcome. We simply just go through the motions. In contrast, when we engage in deliberate practice, we are intentional about our goal and give it our full attention. For example, instead of saying, "I'm going to study now," and opening up a book, we might say to ourselves, "I am going to decide the best way for me to master the knowledge I need for the exam," and then proceed to do so.

WHEN GRIT ISN'T HAPPENING

It's not easy to stick with something long enough to get past the struggle, especially if a student is struggling in a variety of areas. For kids who have ADHD and weaker executive function skills, even in the most ideal work environments and with the most positive supports, it can be so hard for them to do as they are required. We must always keep in mind that "kids do well *if* they can."

As tempting as it may be to try to encourage students with positive statements and to dangle the possibility of rewards, sometimes the best approach is to provide honest, compassionate empathy ("I know this is hard" or "It seems you are feeling frustrated") and to then engage in some detective work with the student. This is where taking a collaborative problem-solving approach is beneficial, as it helps students become aware of their own thinking process and become part of the solution.

The following are some questions that you can ask students (and yourself) as you think about what might be getting in the way:

- Does the present goal make sense?

- Can the goal or activity be broken down into smaller steps?

- What is the story the student is telling themselves about why he or she is not progressing?

- Is there a change that can be made in the environment that would help?

- Is there a need for a break?

- Is hunger or time of day impacting performance?

CAN I JUST MASTER SOMETHING FIRST?

Oftentimes, when students who struggle in the classroom finally begin to feel comfortable with a skill, they are propelled to conquer the next level. Unlike other students, they rarely get to relax and enjoy the sense of accomplishment. For students who have been struggling to succeed and are showing signs of defiance—which can manifest as avoidance as much as active resistance—it is sometimes valuable to allow them to choose ONE class, subject, or goal to put their major energy into. Doing so gives them the opportunity to experience success, rather than having them feel the weight of various competing demands and experiencing subsequent disapproval, disappointment, or failure. **The following worksheet gives students the opportunity to reflect on their learning and develop concrete ideas for their next steps.**

Taking Charge of My Learning

• • •

In your teacher's voice, tell yourself how YOU are doing. Give yourself specific feedback about your homework and exams. Think about your strengths. Are you using these to complete your homework and prepare for tests?

Subject	What I did to prepare for exams that worked really well	What I did to prepare for exams that wasn't worth doing	What I COULD have done but either forgot or didn't think of until too late	What I CAN do throughout the term to prepare for midterms and finals
Math				
Science				
Social Studies				
English				
Foreign Language				

The following are some steps you can take to help students experience success as they master one thing at a time:

1. Choose with the student an area of skill development that you believe would be beneficial to master. Let it be something that is either of high interest to the student or that is more easily mastered. For example, this could involve organizing baseball cards based on a category (e.g., statistics, state), developing a routine of writing two sentences each day, or practicing typing for 10 minutes each day.

2. Let the goal be the *doing* of the activity.

3. Determine with the student how you will measure success.

4. Ask the student what he or she will gain by staying with the activity to its completion.

5. Allow the student to grade his or her progress.

WHAT DO YOU WANT TO GET BETTER AT?

Earlier in the chapter, we mentioned that we each had a fixed mindset in certain areas of our lives. We have each worked hard to overcome these beliefs about ourselves, and are we grateful we did! We will now share our stories with you and encourage you to find a story from your own life to share with your students as you help them develop grit. Sometimes, the most powerful lessons are the ones we share from our own lives.

Cindy's Story

Growing up, I was not much of an athlete. As an adult, I occasionally rode my bicycle with my children around the neighborhood for a few miles—nothing too strenuous. When I was 48 years old, a friend of mine (who was also not much of an athlete) mentioned that she was training to run a half marathon in Alaska. She had joined "Team in Training," which is an organization that helps raise funds for the Leukemia and Lymphoma Society while helping you train for whatever endurance event you've signed up for.

"Alaska!" I thought, "Wow, so cool." I didn't want to run, though. "No worries," she said, "They have biking events too." "Well, okay!" I thought. So, I signed up on a whim to train for a 100-mile bike ride across Long Island to Montauk. Although my family and I thought it was a crazy idea, I was motivated to raise the money for personal reasons and thought that this could be a great adventure. However the problem was—as I said—I didn't believe I was much of an athlete. In fact, both of my parents had been very heavy cigarette smokers, and I grew up in the days when smoking in the car with the windows up was normal. **The story I told myself was that I did not have the lung capacity and could not be an athlete**.

When I showed up for my first training session with the team, they were already up to riding 35 miles per day! I thought that if I could make it 10 miles, then that would be amazing. However, the coach stayed with me the whole time, giving me specific tips, encouragement, and support. And I made it! 35 miles. Of course, the next day I could barely walk. The next week, we were supposed to do 40 miles. I thought to myself, "Hmm, I did 35. I guess I can do 40." And as the weeks went by, it increased to 45 miles, then 50 miles, so on and so forth—until we were now ready for the big day: 100 miles! I am proud to say that I have now done six century rides, two of them in Lake Tahoe. Yes—up the mountains, and down of course (my favorite!).

How did I develop the grit?

1. **I had a schedule**: I knew I had to show up each week for the training ride and was given a written schedule of how many miles (or hours of spin class) to do each week.

2. **I had my support**: Each week, I was in the presence of other committed people who rode with me, and we had a coach to help us progress in our skills.

3. **I used self-talk statements**: "We ride for those who can't." "People gave me money and expect that I will ride the 100 miles." "Just keep looking at the next tree, the next pole." "This struggle will end. I can stay with it until the next mile." "When I get better at this, I will be able to explore so many more places."

My challenge to all of you out there: If you have never done an endurance event, check your mindset! And if you decide to train for one and need a donation for your charity, feel free to email me (info@PTScoaching.com), and I will gladly sponsor you. Go TEAM!

Carly's Story

As a child, I thought of myself as shy though, I was never satisfied keeping to myself and missing out on conversations with my classmates. I had my close friends, but I was always bothered when I watched how easily it seemed that those around me were able to engage in small talk and make new friends.

My favorite pastime growing up was rock climbing. It was a great environment for me to gain confidence, strength, and connect with others who shared a common interest. My sophomore year of college, I stumbled upon my dream summer job: a counselor at an extreme sports camp for individuals with autism spectrum disorder just outside of Aspen, Colorado. I was studying to be a special education teacher, and I was going to get to teach rock climbing to kids with autism.

Next thing I know, I'm leaving my home in New York for a life-changing summer in "Colorful Colorado." It only took a week working at the camp before I knew that I needed to move to Colorado as soon as I was done with college. **However, the story I told myself was that I was too shy to move across the country completely alone and be happy**. I was the shy kid who didn't make friends very easily and was frequently reminded by others of how quiet I was. But Colorado had mountains, wildflowers, and people who connected to my rock-climber lifestyle. I was terrified, but my mind was set.

I wanted to be able to move to Colorado completely on my own and be okay. I may have been quiet—and I definitely still am—but that didn't mean that I enjoy spending all of my time alone. I didn't know a soul in the state of Colorado, but I was determined to do all of the Skype interviews I needed to get my first teaching job and to find some people I could connect with to create a happy life. Now, five years later, I am loving my fifth year of teaching. I have formed solid friendships, found a romantic partner who makes me happy, and have a wonderful group of people with whom I go rock climbing every weekend. I have found my happy, secure community. Not to mention, my mom just moved here to join me! I have surely created the life I want in the place I love, and I could never see myself leaving.

How did I develop the grit?

1. **I had my support system:** I am blessed with incredibly supportive parents who knew as well as I did that this was the right choice for me, and they helped me make it happen. I also have friends who would miss me but who still assured me that this was the right choice for me.

2. **I never let myself look back:** I visualized what I truly wanted for myself and kept checking items off my to-do list that led me toward my goal.

3. **I reframed my shyness and learned to enjoy my introverted self:** I am still that quiet person in most rooms, but I learned to both appreciate and embrace my introversion. The more I accepted who I was, the more confidence I gained, and the less I allowed my quiet nature to get in the way of creating my happiness.

My advice to all of you out there: Follow that crazy dream, even when no one else around you is trying to do anything similar.

7.
The Power of Student Goal Setting

INTENTIONAL GOAL SETTING: STACK TITLES ENGAGING STUDENTS IN THEIR OWN LEARNING

We all have ambitions and aspirations that drive us. For students, these aspirations can be overheard in the halls, in their homes, and inside their heads:

- "I'm going to get all A's this year.'"
- "I'm going to make the baseball team."
- "I'm going to make new friends."
- "I'm not going to get in any fights this year."
- "I won't let myself be bullied this year."

However, without a well-thought-out, detailed plan, these statements are nothing more than a dream, bravado, or magical thinking. Perhaps they are expressing desires, or reflecting other people's expectations of them. **Dreams are things we want, whereas goals are our plan to make things happen: the pathway from the starting point to the end point.**

Our aim in teaching goal setting is to give students the rationale, structure, and support they need to develop this vital life skill. As we discussed in Chapter 6, the first step in this process involves teaching students about a growth mindset and helping them develop grit through deliberate practice. However, the next step in goal setting involves helping students identify their desired goals and bring them to fruition. Helping them experience the power of choosing life with intention, rather than relying on chance.

By teaching students *how* to set goals, we are providing them with a tremendous gift that they will be able to use their whole lives. As with any lesson, the more that you can weave in your own life experiences into a discussion of goal setting, the greater the message you can deliver to your students. When helping students learn about goals, think of examples from your own life when you accomplished something and how the process of achievement began.

A GOAL
WITHOUT A PLAN
IS JUST A WISH

In this chapter, we describe the following points to help you best teach your students about the power of student goal setting:

1. Why goal setting is important
2. How to set effective goals
3. Steps toward achieving goals
4. Dealing with barriers and obstacles
5. Monitoring progress

WHY IS GOAL SETTING IMPORTANT?

A *goal* is something that we want to achieve so much that we are willing to plan and work toward making that desire a reality. Setting goals is important because it helps us to focus our energy, develop our plans, live our life with intention, and recognize our accomplishments. Learning to set specific, attainable goals is a life skill that takes time, experimentation, and experience.

Helping students learn the process of intentional goal setting and helping them work toward achieving those goals is beneficial:

- Goal setting involves using the executive functions to plan, organize, initiate, and track one's progress toward that goal. It also requires utilizing self-talk to direct future plans.
- Intentionally setting goals empowers students to strive for self-improvement. Students learn to practice using a growth-mindset philosophy as they think about the possibilities in their future.
- Students practice applying grit and perseverance to stay the course.
- Individuals who set goals and work toward them find that not only do they perform better, but they experience less stress and anxiety as a result of knowing their direction and feeling more in control of the outcome.
- People often report that they are happier and more satisfied with their lives when they engage in goal setting.

Even young students can develop a focus and a habit of goal setting. You will be providing your students with a tremendous gift that they will be able to use their whole lives. Remember that when possible and appropriate, you may want to include experiences from your own life to enhance the value of the goal-setting lessons.

Two Types of Goals

There are two primary types of goals toward which people may be working: performance goals and personal development goals. **Performance goals** have to do with *what* students want to achieve. For example, these goals can include the desire to get past a test, to make the baseball team, or to get first place in the science fair. **Personal development goals** have to do with *how* students will achieve those goals. That is, they are goals that are oriented toward the process of learning and mastering new skills. For example, students' personal development goals may be to engage in better time management, get along better with others, and stop procrastinating.

As educators, a primary focus for our students is their performance in school—and their performance is generally measured by their grades. However, as we discussed in Chapter 2, how students perform on various measures of achievement is not only dependent on what they know; it's also a reflection of the *process* they use when taking tests and doing their work. Therefore, helping students become aware of *how* they can improve the process by which they learn (and then setting goals related to these factors) will ultimately help improve their performance.

We all have thoughts about the things that we would like to achieve. In order to begin teaching students about goal setting, it is important to help them recognize the goals and dreams that they already think about, even if they do not yet have a specific plan. Don't focus yet on when these goals are to be accomplished; instead, just focus on the free thought of what they hope for their future. For some, it may be playing on a particular sports team in school or being in the band. For others, it may involve being in the movies or publishing a book. Or perhaps they may be focused on learning a new skill, such as riding a bicycle or playing an instrument. We want to encourage the conversation to be centered around personal development goals at first so that they are not focused on the achievements themselves.

The following two worksheets are intended to help students begin the process of setting goals by identifying what they want to achieve in their future, and then identifying how they can improve the skills needed to achieve that goal. First, have each student complete the "What's in My Future?" worksheet. Allow them to keep their sheet private so that they can feel free to express their dreams and goals without concern for others' judgments or critiques. This activity is meant to get students excited about the process of making wonderful things happen in their lives and will help them choose their performance goal. Once students internalize the concept of looking at goals as real possibilities toward which to work, they can start taking the needed steps to achieve those goals. In order for the activity to feel more tangible, you may need to help students come up with a timeframe for completing certain goals that is within a period that you can monitor. This may mean helping them break down a larger goal into some smaller goals or steps that can be accomplished during that specified time.

Then, have each student complete the "Expanding My Wheel" worksheet. This exercise helps students evaluate their skills in *how* they approach their learning and performance in school. The worksheet lists several common areas where students may need to work on strengthening their skills. Depending on their age and their awareness of their skills, you may choose to fill in each of the sections for them or let them decide what they want to include. This activity is intended to help students choose their personal development goal.

> "You have brains in your head.
> You have feet in your shoes.
> You can steer yourself
> any direction you choose.
> You're on your own.
> And you know what you know.
> And YOU are the one who'll decide where to go..."
> – Dr. Seuss

What's in My Future?

· · ·

When you daydream or let your mind wander, do you ever think about what you hope to be doing, enjoying, participating in, or experiencing at any point in the future? How awesome would it be to make those thoughts a reality?

On the chart below, list 10 things that you would like to have in your future. Try to choose some things that you want to happen very soon, and some that you want to happen later on. Then, write down when you would like to have these things happen.

What do I want to do, enjoy, participate in, or experience?	When do I want this to happen?
1.	
2.	
3.	
4.	
5.	
6.	
7.	
8.	
9.	
10.	

Expanding My Wheel

• • •

Being able to perform well in school is not just about knowing the facts. It's also about being able to *show* that you know the information you've learned. The best way to do this is by improving your executive function skills, which are the skills that help you do what you need to do to reach your goals.

On the next page is a wheel that has eight labeled segments and five numbered circles. For each segment of the wheel, ask yourself, "How well do I think I am performing in this area?" The center of the wheel represents "NOT SATISFIED" (1 point), and the outer edge represents "EXTREMELY SATISFIED" (5 points). Rank your level of satisfaction with each segment by lightly coloring in each part of the segment that represents your current level of satisfaction. Then, rate your overall satisfaction with your performance by summing up the numbers in each segment.

Here is the challenge: Your total value may not add up to more than 40 points, and you may not have less than 15 points. That is okay! We all have areas in our lives that we need to improve, and we all have things that we are great at! Once you have completed your wheel, you will be able to set appropriate goals to help you improve your performance skills.

Expanding My Wheel

...

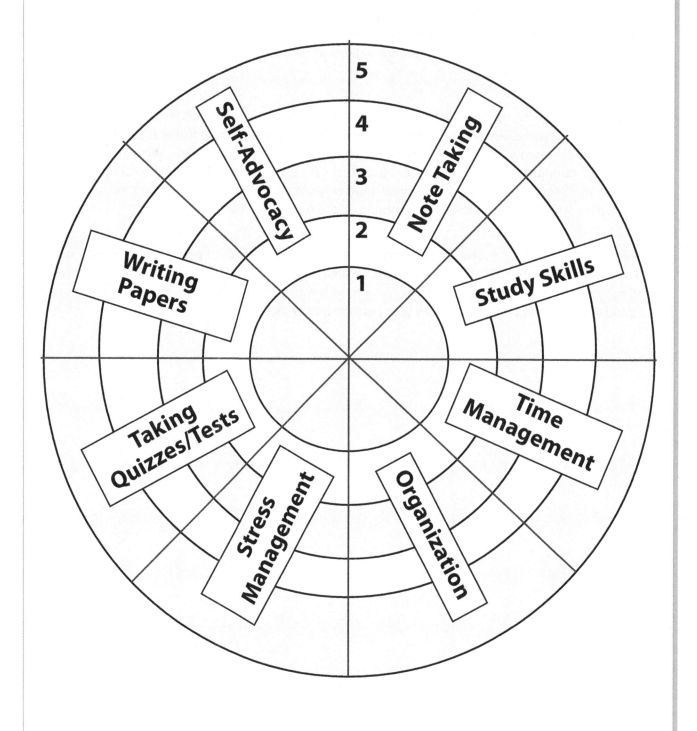

Choosing a Goal

Choosing to pursue a goal is a very powerful commitment. It takes time, effort, and—sometimes—additional resources. **How do we improve the potential of achieving our goals? We write them down**. Indeed, research by Dr. Gail Matthews, a psychology professor at the Dominican University in California, found that people who write down their goals are significantly more likely to achieve them than those who do not. To be more specific: She found that individuals who write their goals down are 42% more likely to achieve them!

Writing down our goals makes us more likely to achieve them because actively forming the words forces us to narrow in on exactly what we want to accomplish and come up with a specific plan and strategy by which to achieve this goal. In addition, the act of writing helps us store the information in our long-term memory—a different part of the brain. The written work also serves as a visual reminder, especially helpful for people with ADHD and executive function challenges who may struggle with working memory, organization, and focus.

When you help students think about choosing a goal, you want to know what their motivation is behind that goal. Are they driven because the goal is something that they feel in their gut? Is it something that they are excited to achieve? Or, it is more of a means to an end? Something that, once completed, will open opportunities, or make life easier or more enjoyable. **The following worksheet is intended to help students pin down what specific performance and personal development goals they would like to achieve and why they would like to achieve these goals.**

> "When I write a goal down—and I truly write
> them down—it becomes a part of me.
> That's a contract that I sign with myself to say,
> 'I don't care what happens—I'm going to stay on this path.
> I'm going to try and see this through;
> I'm going to give it my best shot, my best effort.'"
> —Gail Devers

Choosing a Goal

· · ·

On the "What's in My Future" worksheet, you gave some thoughts about things in your life that you would like to achieve, participate in, or experience. These are known as your **performance goals.** On the "Expanding My Wheel" worksheet, you assessed how satisfied you are with the executive functioning skills that you use to help you succeed in your schoolwork. The skills that you would like to improve upon reflect your **personal development goals.**

Looking over your answers on each of these worksheets, choose one goal from each worksheet that you are most drawn to, and write it below.

Performance Goal: _____

Personal Development Goal: _____

After you have selected a performance goal and a personal development goal, answer the following questions.

Performance Goal

1. Why is this goal important to you?

_____

_____

2. What are the benefits for you in reaching this goal?

_____

_____

3. What do you want to be different about your life?

_____

_____

4. How will you know that you achieved this goal? What will be different?

_____

_____

5. How will you feel once you have achieved this goal?

_____

_____

Now that you have answered these questions, are you ready to commit to your goal? If, after completing this exercise, you want to go back and revise your performance goal, go for it! Setting and achieving goals is a lifelong skill that takes time to develop.

_____ I am ready to commit to my goal.

_____ I am going to choose a different goal from my worksheet.

Personal Development Goal

1. Why is this goal important to you?

_____

_____

2. What are the benefits for you in reaching this goal?

_____

_____

3. What do you want to be different about your life?

_____

_____

4. How will you know that you achieved this goal? What will be different?

_____

_____

5. How will you feel once you have achieved this goal?

_____

_____

Now that you have answered these questions, are you ready to commit to your goal? If, after doing this exercise, you want to go back and revise your personal development goal, go for it! Setting and achieving goals is a lifelong skill that takes time to develop.

_____ I am ready to commit to my goal.

_____ I am going to choose a different goal from my worksheet.

Finding the Motivation to Commit

Students and adults can often struggle to find the inspiration and motivation to get started on their goals. Students who have ADHD may find this especially challenging since they have often experienced so much disappointment, either personally or in the eyes of others, when they have fallen short of expectations they felt they could or should have achieved.

The "Finding Your Inspiration" worksheet is intended to help students develop the motivation to commit to their goals. The worksheet helps students foster their own drive and commitment by asking them to consider how other well-known and inspiring figures in the field have achieved their own goals. Following this worksheet, you'll also find a list of inspirational quotes that you can give to students to help them find the motivation and inspiration to get started.

Finding Your Inspiration

• • •

Throughout history, people have overcome obstacles large and small to achieve amazing things. Sometimes, the achievements are private, personal triumphs, such as overcoming a fear of speaking to a new group of people. Sometimes, the achievements are public and grand, such as creating a new company, winning a major competition, or discovering a significant scientific advancement. Learning about how others have found their inspiration and achieved their goals can be helpful in stimulating your own drive and commitment.

Below is a list of famous people who have achieved significant accomplishments in their lives:

Nelson Mandela	Michael Jordan
Chris Gardner	Jim Carrey
Oprah Winfrey	Steven Spielberg
Richard Branson	Nick Vujicic
Michael Phelps	Frederick Douglass
Helen Keller	Tony Robbins
Ludwig van Beethoven	Victor Frankl
Albert Einstein	Bethany Hamilton

After researching some of the names above, circle one person from the list, and then answer the following questions about him or her:

1. What obstacles or challenges did this person face?

_____

_____

_____

_____

2. What is an accomplishment that this person achieved in spite of the challenges he or she faced?

_____

_____

_____

_____

3. What are three quotes from this person that you find inspiring?

_____

_____

_____

_____

4. Choose one of these quotes and write 3–5 sentences that describe why this quote appeals to you and what you can do to remind yourself of its inspiration.

_____

_____

_____

_____

_____

_____

_____

_____

Inspirational Quotes

. . .

The following are a few great inspirational quotes to help you get motivated toward committing to your goal.

"A dream becomes a goal when action is taken toward its achievement."

— Bo Bennett, businessman

"Desire is the key to motivation, but it's determination and commitment to an unrelenting pursuit of your goal—a commitment to excellence—that will enable you to attain the success you seek."

— Mario Andretti, champion race car driver

"Focused, hard work is the real key to success. Keep your eyes on the goal, and just keep taking the next step towards completing it. If you aren't sure which way to do something, do it both ways and see which works better."

— John Carmack, computer programmer, engineer, and businessman

"Obstacles are those frightful things you see when you take your eyes off your goal."

— Henry Ford, founder of Ford Motor Company

"I visualized where I wanted to be, what kind of player I wanted to become. I knew exactly where I wanted to go, and I focused on getting there."

— Michael Jordan, NBA All Star and winner of six NBA championships

"Do not be embarrassed by your failures. Treat failure as a lesson on how not to approach achieving a goal, and then use that learning to improve your chances of success when you try again. Failure is only the end if you decide to stop."

— Sir Richard Branson, businessman and philanthropist

"Do the one thing you think you cannot do. Fail at it. Try again. Do better the second time. The only people who never tumble are those who never mount the high wire."

— Oprah Winfrey, media mogul and philanthropist

"A man without a goal is like a ship without a rudder."

— Thomas Carlyle, philosopher

"When you put a lot of hard work into one goal, and you achieve it, that's a really good feeling."

— Derek Jeter, MBA All Star

"I can never be safe; I always try and go against the grain. As soon as I accomplish one thing, I just set a higher goal. That's how I've gotten to where I am."

— Beyoncé Knowles, Grammy-Award-winning musician

"Do not be embarrassed by your failures, learn from them and start again."

— Sir Richard Branson, businessman and philanthropist

"The greater danger for most of us isn't that our aim is too high and we miss it, but that it is too low and we reach it."

— Michelangelo, artist

"The future belongs to those who believe in the beauty of their dreams."

— Eleanor Roosevelt, former First Lady, diplomat, and activist

"Aim for the moon. If you miss, you may hit a star."

— W. Clement Stone, businessman and philanthropist

"There will be obstacles. There will be doubters. There will be mistakes. But with hard work, there are no limits."

— Michael Phelps, Olympic champion swimmer

"Why should you continue going after your dreams? Because seeing the look on the faces of the people who said you couldn't… will be priceless."

— Kevin Ngo, writer

"When I feel tired, I just think about how great I will feel once I finally reach my goal."

— Michael Phelps, Olympic champion swimmer

"A goal is a dream with a deadline."

—Napoleon Hill, writer

"You can, you should, and if you're brave enough to start, you will."

—Stephen King, writer

"If you don't make the time to work on creating the life that you want, you're going to spend a lot of time dealing with a life you don't want."

— Kevin Ngo, writer

"By recording your dreams and goals on paper, you set in motion the process of becoming the person you most want to be. Put your future in good hands — your own."

— Mark Victor Hansen, writer

HOW TO SET EFFECTIVE GOALS: MAKE THEM "SMART"

For a goal to be more than a dream or a wish, we want to make sure that it qualifies as a "SMART" goal. That is, the goal must be **S**pecific, **M**easurable, **A**ttainable, **R**elevant, and **T**ime-Bound. Using this SMART acronym can help students develop more effective goals by teaching them to evaluate both the merit and the wording of their goal.

In order for a goal to be **specific**, students must define the goal in as much detail as possible with positive, powerful language. The more that students can visualize their goal, the more they are able to stay focused on accomplishing it. In order to make sure that a goal is specific, students need to ask themselves *what* exactly they want to accomplish, *who* needs to be involved in order to achieve the goal, and (if relevant) *where* they will accomplish this goal.

A goal must also be **measurable** so that students can know when their goal has been accomplished. By breaking down goals into measurable parts, students can track their progress and determine when they have achieved set deadlines along the way. Additionally, in order for a goal to be **attainable**, it must be reasonable and achievable. We want students to set goals that stretch themselves enough to grow, but we also want to ensure that their goals are realistic. When asking themselves whether or not a goal is attainable, students need to consider whether they have the necessary resources and supports to allow them to reach that goal.

When focusing on whether a goal is **relevant**, students must determine whether the goal is worth their efforts. They should consider why the goal is important to them and whether it is consistent with their values and other long-term goals. Last, effective goals are **time-bound** in that they have a clearly defined time frame for their completion. Setting realistic time frames around a goal is important because open-ended goals tend to be forgotten. Therefore, students must ask themselves when they can realistically plan to accomplish their goal and stick to this time frame.

The following two worksheets are intended to help students get into the habit of developing SMART goals. The first worksheet can be used as guided practice to allow the students to deepen their understanding of how to word effective goals. The second worksheet will give them guidance to begin their goal-writing process.

Turn Your Goals into SMART Goals

· · ·

In order to develop effective goals, you want to make sure that your goals are **SMART**. For example, imagine that your goal is to increase your typing speed. While that *is* a goal, it is not a SMART goal. However, you can turn this goal into a SMART goal by making it **S**pecific, **M**easurable, **A**ttainable, **R**elevant, and **T**ime-bound:

Specific	I will improve my current typing speed to 30 words per minute.
Measurable	I will practice typing for 15 minutes per day and track my progress at the end of each week.
Attainable	I have access to the school's computer lab during study hall where I can practice during the week, and I have a laptop I can use at home.
Relevant	Typing faster will help me express my thoughts more easily and produce higher quality work.
Time-bound	I will improve my typing speed by December 15th.

For this exercise, look at the following examples of goals and help reframe each statement into one that is more targeted and detailed.

Specific	I will do better in math.	
Measurable	I will improve in baseball.	
Attainable	I will eliminate sugar from my diet.	
Relevant	I will be the best tennis player.	
Time-bound	I will write my first book.	

Specific	I will be in better shape.	
Measurable	I will have better study habits.	
Attainable	I will exercise one hour every day.	
Relevant	I will research where I want to live after college.	
Time-bound	I will be a fast typist.	

Specific	I will have more friends.	
Measurable	I will have better friends.	
Attainable	I will get all A's.	
Relevant	I will become a master chef.	
Time-bound	I will study more often.	

My SMART Goals

• • •

Now that you have learned about SMART goals and gotten some practice reframing goals into SMART goals, it is time to apply this concept to your own goals. Refer back to the "Choosing a Goal" worksheet, where you developed a performance goal and a personal development goal.

First, look at the **personal development goal** that you identified and turn that statement into a SMART goal.

1. Write your personal development goal as you had written it on the previous worksheet.

   _____

   _____

2. What is your **specific** goal? What *exactly* will you accomplish?

   _____

   _____

3. How will you know when you have reached your goal? How will you track your progress to **measure** that you have been successful?

   _____

   _____

4. Is this goal **attainable**? It is possible to achieve this goal given your resources and constraints? Explain how you know this is possible.

   _____

   _____

5. Why is this goal worth your efforts? What makes it **relevant** in your life now?

   _____

   _____

6. How is this goal **time-bound**? What is the deadline for completing this goal?

   _____

   _____

7. Now, as you look at each of your SMART statements, reword your original personal development goal so that it includes each "SMART" component.

_____

_____

Then, look at the **performance goal** that you identified and turn that statement into a "SMART" goal too.

1. Write your performance goal as you had written it on the previous worksheet.

_____

_____

2. What is your **specific** goal? What *exactly* will you accomplish?

_____

_____

3. How will you know when you have reached your goal? How will you track your progress to **measure** that you have been successful?

_____

_____

4. Is this goal **attainable**? It is possible to achieve this goal given your resources and constraints? Explain how you know this is possible.

_____

_____

5. Why is this goal worth your efforts? What makes it **relevant** in your life now?

_____

_____

6. How is this goal **time-bound**? What is the deadline for completing this goal?

_____

_____

7. Now, as you look at each of your SMART statements, reword your original performance goal so that it includes each "SMART" component.

_____

_____

STEPS TOWARD ACHIEVING GOALS

Once the students have clearly defined and written their goals, it is vital that they break down each goal into specific, actionable steps. They will also benefit from anticipating the challenges they may face in achieving each component. Especially for students who struggle with focus and organization, having detailed, smaller steps will allow them to visualize and manage the process. **The following "Mapping the Pathway" worksheet will help students break down their goals into specific steps.**

Mapping the Pathway

• • •

To achieve your goal, you need an action plan. That is, a specific road map to get where you want to go in the time that you want to get there. Anticipating each of the steps in advance will help you develop an effective plan. This exercise will help you create the steps necessary to take your goal from statement to action. You will need to use a separate worksheet for each of your goals.

In the box below, write the SMART goal that you developed on the previous "My SMART Goal" worksheet.

Then, write down all of the things that you need to do to make this goal happen. Include the materials you will need, the steps you'll need to take, the location you will do the work, and anything else that might be involved in creating your success. For example, if your goal is to bake an apple pie, you will need to find a recipe, see what items you already have (both for the cooking utensils and the ingredients), make a shopping list of everything you need, choose a time to cook, etc. If you need more room to write your steps, use the back of this sheet.

1. _____

2. _____

3. _____

4. _____

5 _____

6. _____

DEALING WITH BARRIERS AND OBSTACLES

While there will be challenges that can come up unexpectedly when working toward a goal, many of the challenges we all face are due to our existing habits and patterns of behavior.

The following two worksheets are intended to help students better deal with obstacles that might get in their way. The first worksheet asks students to identify potential barriers that might interfere with their ability to achieve their goal, whereas the second worksheet helps them brainstorm ways in which to overcome these barriers.

Potential Barriers: What Might Get in the Way?

• • •

Reaching for new goals is exciting. It can also mean making changes in our habits and our beliefs. Below is a list of some of the potential barriers that may get in the way of achieving your goals. For each statement, rate the degree to which you are concerned that this barrier will interfere with your ability to achieve your goal (1 = very little concern, 2 = some concern, 3 = significant concern). There are also blank spaces at the end of the worksheet for you to add any barriers you may think of that are not already included.

_____ 1. I do not feel knowledgeable enough about the material.

_____ 2. I do not have a system in place to organize the work or materials.

_____ 3. I do not have a good awareness of the passage of time or the time commitment that this goal requires.

_____ 4. I experience stress and/or anxiety whenever I approach the steps needed to achieve this goal.

_____ 5. I am overwhelmed by what is involved in order to achieve this goal.

_____ 6. I have difficulty managing the amount of time I spend on social media, texting, talking, and web surfing.

_____ 7. I am easily distracted by others.

_____ 8. I lack self-confidence.

_____ 9. I am anxious about how others will judge me.

_____ 10. I have difficulty getting started and tend to procrastinate.

_____ 11. I have difficulty staying motivated.

_____ 12. I am afraid of failing.

_____ 13. I have difficulty asking others for help.

_____ 14. _____

_____ 15. _____

_____ 16. _____

Battling Potential Barriers

• • •

Review your answers on the "Potential Barriers" worksheet, and choose the top three potential barriers that might get in the way of achieving your goal. Write each potential barrier in the spaces provided, and then write two or three things that you can do to help you overcome that barrier to ensure that you are ready to realize your goal. Sometimes it is easier to imagine how you might help a friend overcome the same obstacle.

Barrier #1: _____

How I will battle the barrier:

_____

_____

_____

Barrier #2: _____

How I will battle the barrier:

_____

_____

_____

Barrier #3: _____

How I will battle the barrier:

_____

_____

_____

MONITORING PROGRESS

Once a goal has been clearly defined, the steps have been identified, and the potential barriers and obstacles have been explored and addressed, it will be vital to help the students stay connected to their goals and on track with their plan. Keep in mind that especially for students who have ADHD, once the initial excitement of creating the plan wears off, it is vital to help them revisit and address each challenge they face along the way. It's also important to help them acknowledge and appreciate the success along the way to help them stay motivated. **The "Support and Accountability" worksheet is intended to increase students' goal commitment by asking them to identify who they can share their goals with and who can hold them accountable in working toward their goals.**

While you may be part of their accountability team, it can be beneficial for their personal growth to experience supporting others as they also receive support. They can gain skills by helping others manage the challenges and obstacles that come up.

Support and Accountability

• • •

Support

Writing down our goals is a very powerful way of helping us define and specify what we want to accomplish. Another way to help us commit to our goals is to speak them out loud to someone else. Whether it's a parent, teacher, coach, or good friend, we all can benefit from knowing someone that is cheering us on when we venture into new challenges or face difficult tasks.

Give some thought about the goals that you want to achieve. Who would be a person you can share the goal with? You may even want to choose someone who plans on working on a similar goal so that you can support one another with tools, resources, and strategies specific to your venture. For each type of goal that you set, you may want to choose a different person with which to share your intention.

I will share my performance goal with _____

I will share my personal development goal with _____

Accountability

To increase your potential for achieving your goal, set aside a regular time to speak to an "accountability partner." This is a person with whom you will share your goal, as well as the specific short-term action steps that you will be taking on a daily or weekly basis. It can be a brief check-in in person, on the phone, or via email. Make sure that you schedule each meeting well in advance so that the business of life does not take over.

Dates and times I will meet with my accountability partner	Dates and times I will meet with my accountability partner
1.	1.
2.	2.
3.	3.
4.	4.
5.	5.
6.	6.
7.	7.

PUTTING IT ALL TOGETHER

Once students have identified a SMART goal, examined the steps needed to achieve that goal, and developed a plan for possible barriers that might get in the way, it's time for them to put it all together in one place. **On the following page is an "Action Plan" worksheet that you can give to students in order to help them synthesize everything they have learned with regard to goal setting. A sample action plan is provided first, followed by a blank action plan that students can fill out with regard to their own goal.**

My Action Plan

. . .

Looking at the steps that you identified on the "Mapping the Pathway" worksheet, take each step and write it in the chart on page 185. These steps should be written down *in the most logical order that they need to be completed.* If the order for a particular step does not matter, or if it is a step that must be done throughout the process, then write down those steps first. The following chart includes a sample action plan.

My SMART Goal: I will improve my current typing speed to 30 words per minute by December 15th. Typing faster will help me express my thoughts more easily and produce higher quality work.

Measurable step I need to take.	How long will it take?	When must it be done by?	What support will I need and from whom?	What challenges might get in the way?
1. Find the best program to practice	1 hour	September 17	Google search and teacher recommendations	Getting distracted during Google search
2. Plan a regular time to practice 30 minutes per day, four days per week	15 minutes	September 22	Check with parents about activities each week	Not putting aside time to practice or marking it as homework; practice time might differ each week
3. Take a baseline typing test to see my current speed	30 minutes	September 27	Google search and teacher recommendations	Getting frustrated if my speed is slower than I thought
4. Start practicing four days a week	2 hours	Begin October 1	None—I can do this myself	Allowing distractions; not including practice as part of real homework
5. Test my progress every four weeks	30 minutes	October 29 November 26 December 15	None—I can do this myself	Getting discouraged if I don't see improvement

I will celebrate my goal achievement by: Buying myself a new baseball mitt.

My action steps to overcome my challenges are:

1. I will set a timer when I am on Google.

2. On Sunday nights, I will look at my schedule for the coming week and write down four dates for my practice time.

3. I will remind myself that getting faster will take practice and that each time, it will get easier.

4. I will remind myself why this goal is important to me. I will hang a picture of a baseball mitt on my wall for encouragement.

5. I will evaluate if I am doing what I intended to do when practicing. I will ask for a good typist to sit with me.

My Action Plan

• • •

My SMART Goal:

_____

_____

Measurable step I need to take.	How long will it take?	When must it be done by?	What support will I need and from whom?	What might get in the way?
1.				
2.				
3.				
4.				
5.				

I will celebrate my goal achievement by: _____

My action steps to overcome my challenges are:

1. _____

2. _____

3. _____

4. _____

5. _____

"You're off to great places!
Today is your day!
Your mountain is waiting,
So... get on your way!"
— Dr. Seuss

CAREER DEVELOPMENT: IT'S NEVER TOO EARLY

As parents and teachers, we recognize that what we learned in the classroom setting is not always directly relevant to our adult lives. As students mature, many of them begin to struggle to say motivated in school since they do not see the connection between what they are learning now and how this relates to their future. For example, students who do not enjoy math (and who do not understand how higher-level math concepts are relevant to their lives) may resist putting in the effort needed to master the concepts they are being taught. Indeed, as a parent coach, my clients often report that their children don't seem to be motivated to do their work no matter what incentives they are offered. However, the *skills and techniques* that we learned in the classroom often do transfer to new situations and opportunities in our adult lives. For example, while we may not see how performing a specific science experiment will help us in the future, the process of investigation, tracking, synthesizing results, and explaining our findings is a set of skills that requires time and practice to master.

Our goal as educators and parents is to help students keep the doors to future opportunities wide open. One of the greatest goals that most people face is deciding what type of work they will pursue once they finish school. The best way address this challenge is to help students understand the vast world of career possibilities and the various pathways people take in pursuing, and often creating, their careers.

When asked, most adults can only speak about two or three careers with any true knowledge—perhaps their own, their parents', and their partner's. Similarly, students are often only aware of the jobs that they are immediately exposed to. If we can broaden their knowledge and understanding of a wide range of careers, this will allow them to expand their view of their future possibilities.

In the two handouts that follow, we encourage students to interview adults to learn about what is involved in a range of careers. The first worksheet is meant for elementary school grades. It creates an opportunity for students to learn about a range of careers outside of what they are exposed to in their immediate world. **The second worksheet is geared toward students in middle school and high school.** At this point, many students begin to feel that they should know what they want to do as adults, and those who don't often feel distraught, discouraged, or even anxious. For these students, the prospect of college becomes a time of great conflict and confusion. We want these students to see that not everyone knows what they want to pursue after school and that many adults find their passion and success after having tried a few different pathways. The important idea is to keep their options open and their minds growing at all times.

Of note, both of these handouts ask students to give their classmates a brief oral presentation summarizing what they have learned. We believe that the oral presentation is an important component of these exercises for two reasons: First, by sharing what they have learned with their classmates, students have an opportunity to reflect and deepen their learning. Second, it gives classmates an opportunity to learn about additional careers that they may not have thought of or learned about.

What Do You Do for Work?

· · ·

When you are in school, playing after school, and even sleeping at night, many of the adults in your life are busy going to work. Some work as doctors, storekeepers, garbage collectors, or teachers—to name a few. Many work in offices, factories, or even airplanes in the sky—and you may never get to see the kind of work they do all day.

One day in the future, you will also choose what type of work you will want to do. And the best way to choose the type of work that you'll enjoy most is to learn about many different options. In this activity, you'll interview two different adults in your life about the type of work that they do and then share what you have learned with your class.

Instructions:

1. Choose two adults you can have a 10-minute conversation with, either in person or over the phone. These adults can be family members, family friends, or people doing work that you find fun or interesting. When you reach out to them, be clear about what it is that you'd like to talk to them about and why. For example, you might say: "I am interested in learning about different careers. Would you mind speaking with me for about 10 minutes about the work that you do?"

2. For each person that you talk to, ask the following questions. Feel free to add any other questions that you may think of.

   • What is your job title?

   • How long have you been doing this job?

   • What kinds of things do you do at your job?

   • What is the best thing about your job?

   • What part do you like the least?

3. Prepare a two-minute presentation for your classmates where you can share what you have learned. Feel free to include a photo of the person at their place of work if that is possible.

4. Write a simple thank you note to the people with whom you spoke. In your note, let them know that you appreciated their time and share with them one or two things that you learned.

What Led You to This Career?

• • •

As young children, some people think about what they want to "be" when they grow up, and in rare cases, they end up pursuing that actual career. However, most adults today are in careers that they did not necessarily envision when they were younger.

It is not always easy to see how the work that adults do is related to what they studied in school and perhaps even college. However, all the learning that we do contributes to the adults we become and the opportunities we have in life. During this activity, you will be interviewing two adults to learn about what led them to the work they are doing today.

Instructions:

1. Choose two people to interview about their work. These should be adults in jobs that you know little or nothing about so that you are exposed to new types of work. You should also choose two people whose work is unrelated to one another. When you reach out to them, be clear upfront about your intention and request. For example, you might say: "I am interested in learning about different careers. Would you mind speaking with me for about 10 minutes about the work that you do?"

2. For each person that you interview, ask the following questions as conversation starters. Based upon their answers, you may want to ask them follow-up questions that allow you to gain a deeper understanding of their work, their choices in pursuing that work, and how they feel about their line of work.

   - What is your job title?

   - How long have you been doing this job?

   - What are your primary responsibilities?

   - How did you decide to pursue this work?

   - Did you have any jobs or careers before this?

   - What prepared you the most for doing this work?

   - What advice do you have for someone who wants to do your job?

3. Prepare a five-minute presentation for your classmates where you can share what you have learned. Feel free to include a photo of the person at their place of work if that is possible.

4. Write a simple thank you note to the people with whom you spoke. In your note, let them know that you appreciated their time and share with them one or two things that you learned.

CONCLUSION

We hope you have gained new insights, tools, and strategies to support children who may think and learn differently. When you find yourself faced with a challenging situation with a student, whether it is helping him learn to manage his need to move about, her frustration with demanding assignments, his difficulty getting started, or any other behaviors that create stress for you, the student, or others in the class, try to take a step back and wonder: "Why is this student having a hard time meeting this specific expectation?" For example, could it be due to the time of day, environment, level of work, or negative self-talk? Kids generally do want to succeed, not stick out, and not get in trouble. They just don't always have the skills they need at the moment to express their challenges, feel safe being vulnerable, or have the knowledge of how to appropriately address their challenges. Engage them in a non-judgmental discussion where together you can be detectives in exploring how to address the issues. Seek the input of those around you for additional perspectives and strategies. Be patient and persistent in pursuing a resolution to the issues, knowing that each day they are maturing and evolving.

References

For your convenience, purchasers can download and print
worksheets and handouts from www.pesi.com/ADHDEF

American Psychiatric Association. *Diagnostic and statistical manual of mental disorders: DSM-5.* (2013). Arlington, VA.

Barkley, R. A., Koplowitz, S., Anderson, T., & McMurray, M. B. (1997). Sense of time in children with ADHD: Effects of duration, distraction, and stimulant medication. Retrieved from https://www.ncbi. nlm.nih.gov/pubmed/9260445.

Blackwell, L. S., Trzesniewski, K. H., & Dweck, C. S. (2007). Implicit theories of intelligence predict achievement across an adolescent transition: A longitudinal study and an intervention. *Child Development, 78*(1), 246-263. doi:10.1111/j.1467-8624.2007.00995.x

Brown, T. (2008). *Attention deficit disorder: The unfocused mind in children and adults.* Connecticut: Yale University Press.

Centers for Disease Control and Prevention. (2018, September 28). National prevalence of ADHD and treatment: New statistics for children and adolescents, 2016. Retrieved from https://www.cdc.gov/ ncbddd/adhd/features/national-prevalence-adhd-and-treatment.html

Coghill, D. R., & Hogg, K. M. (2012). Molecular genetics of attention deficit-hyperactivity disorder (ADHD). *ELS.* doi:10.1002/9780470015902.a0006012.pub2

Cortese, S., & Castellanos, F. X. (2012). Neuroimaging of attention-deficit/hyperactivity disorder: current neuroscience-informed perspectives for clinicians. *Current Psychiatry Reports, 14*(5), 568-578. doi:10.1007/s11920-012-0310-y

Dominican University of California. (n.d.). Study focuses on strategies for achieving goals, resolutions. Retrieved from https://www.dominican.edu/dominicannews/study-highlights-strategies-for-achieving-goals

Duckworth, A. (2018). *Grit: The power of passion and perseverance.* New York: Scribner.

Dupaul, G. J., Gormley, M. J., & Laracy, S. D. (2012). Comorbidity of LD and ADHD. *Journal of Learning Disabilities, 46*(1), 43-51. doi:10.1177/0022219412464351

Dweck, C. S. (2016). *Mindset: the new psychology of success.* New York: Ballantine Books.

Faraone, S. V., Perlis, R. H., Doyle, A. E., Smoller, J. W., Goralnick, J. J., Holmgren, M. A., & Sklar, P. (2005). Molecular genetics of attention-deficit/hyperactivity disorder. *Biological Psychiatry. 57*(11), 1313-1323. doi:10.1016/j.biopsych.2004.11.024

Faraone, S. V., Asherson, P., Banaschewski, T., Biederman, J., Buitelaar, J. K., Ramos-Quiroga, J. A., & Franke, B. (2015). Attention-deficit/hyperactivity disorder. *Nature Reviews (Disease Primers).* Retrieved from https://www.nature.com/articles/nrdp201520.

Goldrich, Cindy, and Babette Rothschild. *8 Keys to Parenting Children with ADHD.* W.W. Norton & Company, 2015.

Greene, R. W. (2014). *The explosive child: A new approach for understanding and parenting easily frustrated, chronically inflexible children.* New York: HarperCollins.

Hallowell, E. M., Hallowell, S., & Orlov, M. (2011). *Married to distraction: How to restore intimacy and strengthen your partnership in an age of interruption.* New York: Ballantine Books Trade Paperbacks.

Hassed, C. (2015). *Mindful learning: Reduce stress and improve brain performance for effective learning.* Colorado: Shambhala Publications.

Mueller, C. M., & Dweck, C. S. (1998). Praise for intelligence can undermine children's motivation and performance. *Journal of Personality and Social Psychology, 75*(1), 33-52. doi:10.1037//0022-3514.75.1.33

Naglieri, J. A., & Goldstein, S. (2014). Using the Comprehensive Executive Function Inventory (CEFI) to assess executive function: From theory to application. In S. Goldstein and J. A. Naglieri (Eds.), *Handbook of executive functioning* (4th ed., 223-244). New York: Springer.

Ramtekkar, U. P., Reiersen, A. M., Todorov, A. A., & Todd, R. D. (2010). Sex and age differences in attention-deficit/hyperactivity disorder symptoms and diagnoses: Implications for *DSM-V* and ICD-11. *Journal of the American Academy of Child & Adolescent Psychiatry, 49*(3) 217-228. doi:10.1016/j.jaac.2009.11.011

Rosier, T. (2014, August 1). *Perspective taking—an important skill.* Retrieved from https://www.adhdcoaches.org/perspective-taking-an-important-skill/

Rubin, G. (2018). *The happiness project: Or, why I spent a year trying to sing in the morning, clean my closets, fight right, read Aristotle, and generally have more fun.* New York: Harpercollins.

Shaw, P., Eckstrand, K., Sharp, W., Blumenthal, J., Lerch, J. P., Greenstein, D., … Rapoport, J. L. (2007). Attention-deficit/hyperactivity disorder is characterized by a delay in cortical maturation. *Proceedings of the National Academy of Sciences, 104*(49), 19649-19654. doi:10.1073/pnas.0707741104

Made in the USA
Coppell, TX
05 October 2022

84141901R00118